How to be a ghost HUNTER

About the Author

Richard Southall (West Virginia) has been interested in the paranormal since a very young age. He currently has degrees in journalism and psychology. His work has appeared in numerous local and national magazines and newspapers, including *Fate* magazine. He enjoys photography, writing, the outdoors, blues music, and the paranormal. Richard is currently in the process of writing two more books, one a collection of short stories, and the other on a West Virginia topic.

To Write to the Author

If you wish to contact the author or would like more information about this book, please write to the author in care of Llewellyn Worldwide and we will forward your request. Both the author and publisher appreciate hearing from you and learning of your enjoyment of this book and how it has helped you. Llewellyn Worldwide cannot guarantee that every letter written to the author can be answered, but all will be forwarded. Please write to:

Richard Southall
℅ Llewellyn Worldwide
P.O. Box 64383, Dept. 0-7387-0312-5
St. Paul, MN 55164-0383, U.S.A.

Please enclose a self-addressed stamped envelope for reply,
or $1.00 to cover costs. If outside U.S.A., enclose
international postal reply coupon.

Many of Llewellyn's authors have websites with additional information and resources. For more information, please visit our website at:
http://www.llewellyn.com

Richard Southall

Llewellyn Publications
St. Paul, Minnesota , U.S.A.

First Edition
Third Printing, 2004

Book design by Michael Maupin
Cover design by Gavin Dayton Duffy
Cover photo © 2002 by Artcraft Studios, Parkersburg, WV

Library of Congress Cataloging-in-Publication Data
Southall, R. H. (Richard H.), 1972–
    How to be a ghost hunter / R. H. Southall.—1st ed.
      p.   cm.
    Includes biological references and index.
    ISBN 0-7387-0312-5
      1. Ghosts—Research—Methodology. I. Title.

BF1461.S66 2003
133.1'07'2—dc21   2002043352

Llewellyn Publications
A Division of Llewellyn Worldwide, Ltd.
P.O. Box 64383, Dept. 0-7387-0312-5
St. Paul, MN 55164-0383, U.S.A.
www.llewellyn.com

Printed in the United States of America

Dedication and Thanks

My sincere gratitude and thanks goes to a great many people, without whose help this book would not have been possible: Susan Sheppard, Crystal Howard, Laura and Tyler Boyle, Tracy Workman, Myssi Gable, Keith Southall, Kenneth Southall, and Dovie Southall, and to everyone else who submitted a story, offered an idea, or simply endured me through this long process. Special thanks to MAJDA and the International Ghost Hunters' Society (IGHS) for providing some of the photos used.

I would like to dedicate this book to two very special people in my life. First, to my niece and future ghost hunter, Morgan Southall, whose curiosity and imagination was always a delight. Second, I'd like to dedicate this book to my loving fiancée Debra. Her belief and dedication to me was an inspiration. I'm so glad you're in my life! I love you, Gumdrop!

Most of all, I would like to dedicate this book to you, the reader, and future ghost hunter!

Richard Southall
September 2001

CONTENTS

INTRODUCTION
Why a Ghost-Hunting Guide?

Books on the paranormal have been written by a great number of people in recent years. Most of the books on ghosts and spirits can usually be divided into two categories. The first type of book only offers accounts of actual hauntings without giving much of an explanation of what the people involved experienced. While this may be very entertaining reading for a cold night by a warm fire, it doesn't really catch the ambiance of the reality of ghosts and spirits in people's lives. Many of the stories are fictionalized and exaggerated to the point that little of the actual account can be found.

The second type of book is almost the exact opposite, going into the many theories and research studies associated with ghosts and other paranormal visitations. However, by delving into the mechanics of ghosts and spirits, the magic and mystery of the personal accounts is generally lost.

This book has been written from a slightly different perspective. Many people who read books on the paranormal are already familiar with ghosts and the paranormal, so I will not go into detail about many of the famous accounts.

However, I will not make this simply a reference book, either. It is meant to be a handbook for people who have an interest in investigating hauntings. Although I'll relate accounts I have experienced personally or have been told from reliable sources, I use them only to illustrate specific types of phenomena you may encounter. The accounts that I do relate will not dominate the entire text of the book, as it does in many other books on the paranormal.

How I Became a Ghost Hunter

I began my paranormal investigations when I was a teenager by researching my own house, which was very haunted. I lived in rural Jackson County, West Virginia, and people in the area, although friendly and helpful, tended to keep pretty much to themselves and certainly would not discuss things such as ghosts and spirits to just anybody. So, I was on my own to investigate what happened in my hometown during the mid-1980s.

Our family moved to a small farmhouse outside of Ripley, West Virginia, in the early 1980s. Soon after we were settled in, strange things began to happen. At first, small items would appear to be misplaced, only to be found in obvious places up to a month later. During the day, when my mother was alone at home and my brothers and I were at school, she began to hear knocks at the door. Of course, when she went to the door, nobody was there.

On one occasion, my mother was sitting in the living room when the room temperature suddenly became much colder. She heard a noise upstairs, as if somebody wearing heavy boots was stomping around. The sound continued down the stairway, and when it reached the bottom, the stomping immediately stopped. This began to occur at the same time each month for over eight months. Each time the sound would come down the steps, the door would open, and the sound would disappear until the following month, when it began again. My mother was afraid to mention this because she did not want to frighten my brothers and me. Little did she know that we were having our own encounters.

In the early autumn following the first staircase incident, my oldest brother and I were at home on a rainy Saturday afternoon. Suddenly the house began to get much colder (the house was heavily insulated and it was a fairly mild day). The stomping started, the stairway door opened, and—again—nobody was there. My brother took a rifle upstairs to see if anybody had broken into the house, but he could not find anything in the two empty upstairs rooms, which were used for storage. We told our mother when she returned home. That was when she told us about her own experiences.

Later that same month, my mother awoke around 3:00 one morning. Her bedroom was adjacent to the bathroom, and standing in the bathroom doorway was an ominous-looking person dressed in a Civil War uniform. He was very tall and thin, wearing wire-frame glasses. She got out of bed, and as she approached him, the apparition simply disappeared. This was the only real apparition that anybody in the family saw at the house, but over time, the encounters became less and less frequent, and, after a few years, subsided altogether.

These encounters were enough for me to do some checking into the history of the house and the area surrounding it. After doing research, I found that Confederate soldiers had marched through the area where the house now stands. No major battles ever took place there, but despite that, our house apparently had the energy of at least one of the soldiers. As it was one of the first, true hauntings that I investigated, it left a very distinct impression on my views of the paranormal.

Thus began my career in parapsychology. I have learned quite a few tricks and techniques on ghost hunting since those early days, and I plan to share many of them with you in this book.

My First Investigations

As I mentioned, I began my paranormal investigations as a teenager by researching my own house. I was so fascinated by what I discovered that I began to follow up on old legends and stories told to me by neighbors, family, and friends. By the time I was comfortable with how to investigate a haunted area, two of my close high-school friends began to accompany me. Not only did we investigate haunted houses, but we found ourselves in abandoned churches, cemeteries, and other places trying to find and photograph a ghost.

However, one of the most exciting hunts my friends and I participated in was the search for "the Mothman." Growing up less than thirty miles from Point Pleasant, West Virginia, the site of the famous Mothman sightings, we had always heard about the story of a large creature with glowing red eyes and gray batlike wings, terrorizing the small community. Only after we found a copy of John Keel's book *The Mothman Prophesies* did we realize the extent of the story's popularity.

We spent the better part of a month gathering information on the history of Point Pleasant, the TNT area (a dynamite-manufacturing plant thought to be haunted), Mothman, and Chief Cornstalk (who cursed the area shortly before his death) before we even attempted to visit the town for firsthand information. We needed to know what we were up against!

The Battle of Point Pleasant was considered by some to be the first battle of the American Revolution. Fought on October 10, 1774, between the Shawnee Indians and the Long Knives of Virginia, Chief Cornstalk played a pivotal part of the outcome of the battle. After the battle, Cornstalk signed a treaty vowing never to fight a white man again.

In 1777, Cornstalk returned to Point Pleasant to Fort Randolph help out the people living in the fort. When he returned to the fort, he was attacked. With his dying breath, he cursed the Point Pleasant area, saying it would find only sorrow for the next two hundred years. He vowed that Point Pleasant would always be plagued by spirits and bad fortune, and that it would never prosper.

After he died, people soon began to forget about Chief Cornstalk's curse. From November 1966 through December 1967, people in the Point Pleasant area began to see a creature that eventually became known as the "Mothman." It appeared as a very tall man with glowing red eyes and expansive, gray, batlike wings. Soon, the accounts began to draw the attention of reporters from around the world, and Point Pleasant was deluged with people who wanted to see this elusive yet terrifying creature. People began to whisper that the Mothman was a direct result of Cornstalk's curse.

The sightings of the Mothman ceased as suddenly as they began, with the collapse of the Silver Bridge in December 1967. Many people were killed as they crossed the bridge when it collapsed. Some people say that they could see glowing forms floating around the supports of the bridge the night before the collapse. From that day on, Mothman was not seen again in the Point Pleasant area.

The TNT area was a place where explosives were manufactured during the world wars. Since it closed down shortly after the Second World War, very mysterious events began to take place. Lights would be seen above the TNT area at all hours of the day and night. People who entered the site would come out very frightened, refusing to tell others of their experiences. Soon it had the reputation of being haunted. Some accounts report that the TNT area was the place where Mothman was first encountered in 1966. That was the perfect place where three headstrong

The Silver Bridge in Point Pleasant, West Virginia, before its collapse in December 1967.

teenagers who hunted ghosts needed to go! During our visit, we not only heard rattling sounds, but also noticed strong, pungent odors that could not be identified. That, combined with our very active teenage imaginations, was enough to keep us from making a return trip to the area!

Investigating Point Pleasant gave me the opportunity to fine-tune some of my skills. I learned very quickly that a good investigator needed to establish a rapport with people instead of simply asking for information. I learned what to ask and what not to ask in order to build rapport with people to the point that they will share their information.

One problem that I encountered time and again was that during my first few investigations, there were no primers or how-to guides on ghost hunting available anywhere. Even

The aftermath of the Silver Bridge collapse. People claimed to see lights flying around the bridge the night before it was destroyed. Was this tragedy the result of Chief Cornstalk's curse, Mothman, or something entirely different?

requesting books through interlibrary loan was very often futile because of the limited supply of any quality books on the subject. This was before the days of the Internet, so I could not simply log on and do a quick search on ghost hunting.

Only when I left for college did I find any books of real substance. I spent hours in the library, doing research for my private, paranormal studies, in addition to concentrating on my coursework. (My grades were not affected, and I felt that the time I invested was not wasted.) However, even the information I did find was mostly from encyclopedias and reference books. By the time that I had graduated college, I learned enough about ghost hunting to develop my own successful methods for investigating hauntings.

Eventually, my reputation for being a ghost hunter spread to various groups of people in my community. I would receive phone calls from families who would ask me to visit their property because of apparent hauntings. Sometimes, simply by talking with and interviewing the people on the telephone, I would find a more rational explanation of the situation; usually noisy pipes, pranksters, or even overactive imaginations.

Other times, I would be intrigued enough to visit the area in person and conduct an investigation. When I visited I often found that there was a real haunting. I helped as much as I could and explained that, with the exception of a very few cases, ghosts were harmless. I did not work with hostile or demonic spirits, but referred them to one of my colleagues who worked exclusively with this type of phenomena. To this day, I will not work with some of the more malevolent manifestations.

Within a year, I had received over twenty calls from people within a fifty-mile radius of where I lived. I responded to each and every call. Soon, I realized that most of the callers were asking similar questions: "What is a ghost?" "How do I know if my house is haunted?" "How did my house become haunted?" "Is it dangerous?" and "How do I get rid of the ghosts?"

In response, I created a booklet on haunted houses that I gave to people when I initially visited them. It was only a six-page pamphlet, but did a good job in answering many of the questions they had. The investigations continued to become more and more frequent.

Parkersburg, West Virginia

Parkersburg was a very prominent town that became wealthy because of the large deposits of natural gas and oil found in the area. Parkersburg was considered by some to be the "wickedest city along the Ohio River." People came from hundreds of miles away to visit the town, often gambling in the casinos and visiting the now-legendary brothels, such as The Red Onion. There were five vaudeville theaters in town, often attracting acts such as the Singing Midgets (of *The Wizard of Oz* fame) and Harry Houdini. However, despite its prosperity, Parkersburg became a quiet, peaceful town after the supplies of natural gas and oil were depleted. Despite the colorful history of Parkersburg during the nineteenth century, Parkersburg's most famous people lived there nearly a century earlier.

Margaret and Harman Blennerhassett were Irish aristocrats who moved to United States in 1796 and settled in the Parkersburg area two years later. They purchased an hourglass-shaped island on the Ohio River about a mile from downtown Parkersburg. The Blennerhassetts were definitely a sight to see in those days. Both were scholars and loved to spend long, cold evenings sitting in front of the fire reading the works of classic literature such as Plato, Shakespeare, and others. While most people lived in rustic cabins and homes, the Blennerhassetts decided to build a mansion worthy of a plantation on their island. Only the finest of everything would do. Their tastes being extravagant, they had to import many of their amenities, such as books and fine wines, from outside of the mid-Ohio Valley. In addition to building a mansion and bringing their own brand of culture to the area, the Blennerhassetts hosted elaborate parties for the area's aristocracy. A great many rich and famous people visited the Blennerhassetts

The Blennerhassett Mansion on Blennerhassett Island. Many people have seen paranormal occurrences while visiting and camping out on the island.

on occasion, including King Charles X of France, Walt Whitman, and a certain vice president by the name of Aaron Burr. The Blennerhassetts and Burr became very good friends, and formed a plan for a colony in what is now Louisiana. Their plan was soon discovered and the president of the United States sent soldiers to the island to apprehend the traitors in 1806. Burr and Blennerhassett left Margaret on the island to distract the soldiers while they made their escape. Harman Blennerhassett fled to the south, where he started a plantation, and was later reunited with Margaret and their two children.

Today the island is a tourist attraction offering horse-drawn wagon rides, a craft village, a camping area, and a guided tour of a reproduction of the mansion. Many people who have visited the island have seen a woman dressed in white walking along the shore near the campground. Apparently, Margaret used to sit by the shore waiting for her husband to return from nearby Marietta. Often she would be wearing a white dress.

One story in particular is of a writer who was canoeing north along the Ohio River in 1992 collecting stories for a magazine in Pittsburgh. He stopped at the island and set up camp. In the early morning hours, he was awakened by the strong scent of perfume. He went outside to find the origin of the scent and was approached by a beautiful woman in a long, white, flowing gown. Since there was a chill in the air, he motioned for her to sit by him and offered to make her some hot coffee. She simply stared at him and walked backward into the early morning fog. The writer was a bit unnerved by this, but decided to get a few extra hours of sleep.

The writer took a large collection of books wherever he went and had them neatly stored in a knapsack outside his tent. Shortly after falling asleep, he was awakened again by the sound of somebody rustling through his knapsack outside. When the rustling stopped, he opened his tent and was amazed at what he saw. Every book had been taken from his knapsack and neatly stacked on the ground beside the smoldering remains of the campfire. Somebody had been curious about what the writer was reading and decided to look through the collection.

The writer told some people in Parkersburg about it the next day. When he described the woman to the small group of people, they became very still. It turned out that he had described Margaret Blennerhassett perfectly. She was always a bibliophile and could not resist looking at people's books to see if anything piqued her interest. Her love for books had apparently survived the grave. The writer said that he would return to Parkersburg to write a story about his experience, but in over ten years, no one has heard a word from him.

A final note to this haunting took place not too terribly long ago. Margaret's remains were exhumed and returned to Blennerhassett Island, where she was given a proper Christian funeral. Before the funeral, the apparition of a woman in white was fairly common. Since her remains have been returned to the island, no sightings of Margaret have been reported. She always considered Blennerhassett Island her true home. Now that she has been returned, perhaps she is finally at rest.

Parkersburg and the Civil War

In addition to its historical significance, Parkersburg had a very strategic role in the Civil War. Two major rivers, the

Little Kanawha and the Ohio, meet in Parkersburg. These rivers brought troops and supplies to areas throughout the war-torn states. The B&O Railroad also brought wounded soldiers and supplies to one of Parkersburg's five hospitals during the war. Many of the downtown businesses were transformed into makeshift hospitals to accomodate the wounded soldiers sent into the Parkersburg area. In these hospitals, many soldiers met their end. And, as you may expect, there are indeed many ghosts that still haunt those areas.

One of the hospital sites, Quincy Hill, is particularly haunted. Quincy Hill was used as the overflow hospital or waiting area. When the other hospitals were filled to capacity, the wounded soldiers were sent to the hill that overlooks Parkersburg and the Ohio River. In order to receive help, some of the soldiers crawled down the hill into the streets to beg citizens to help them ease their pain. People who have visited Quincy Hill have claimed to hear the sound of somebody moving through the brush and bushes on the hill. On occasion, voices are even heard. Yet, in each and every case, nobody is seen making the sounds.

Haunted Parkersburg

In 1994 I had moved to Parkersburg. I had been there only a few months when in August I was introduced to accomplished author and astrologer Susan Sheppard. Often Susan would appear as a guest on WTAP's *Daybreak* morning television talk show, offering horoscopes to callers. When she wasn't busy doing horoscopes, she was writing her latest book or managing a local group of poets and creative writers. Soon after being introduced to Susan, I called her to get some information on ghosts and spirits for an article I was writing for a local newszine, *The Village Idiot*. We soon found we had a lot in common, and became very good friends.

After returning from a trip to New Orleans, Susan told me about the haunted tours that were given throughout the city. Apparently, she decided to go on one of the tours while visiting. She was not very impressed with some of the stories, and felt that given the opportunity, she could do a better tour. I knew that Parkersburg was a very historical town, with a great influence on the Civil War. I offered to help her dig up some ghost stories from the town's past.

We didn't have to go far before we realized the vast history that was in the mid-Ohio Valley. Immediately after obtaining the historical facts about the area, Susan and I began developing paranormal research for our own tour. We placed ads in local newspapers and magazines for any

Author Susan Sheppard of Haunted Parkersburg tours stands beside the Jackson family grave at Riverview Cemetary. It is said the apparition of a woman resembling the statue monument has been seen walking the cemetary late at night.

ghost stories that people had about the area. Flyers were placed on telephone poles and at bus stops. We went to different prominent historians and gathered as much information on Parkersburg's history and legends as possible. Within days, the calls started pouring in.

The Haunted Parkersburg tour took the mid-Ohio Valley by storm. We were constantly interviewed by the media—newspapers, television and radio reporters, and talk show hosts were contacting us on a weekly basis. They wanted to know if Parkersburg was really haunted, and by the number of reports we were receiving, both Susan and I responded with a resounding "Yes!"

Today, the tours bring over two thousand people annually to the Parkersburg area and the Blennerhassett Hotel, which hosts the tour each year. We have had many paranormal events happen on the tour. Generally, with each tour, we lose power in all of our flashlights, despite the fact that we thoroughly check them before each tour, and have new batteries as backup. We've had cigar smoke appear in mid-air on many occasions when we were telling the story about William Chancellor, the cigar-smoking owner of the Blennerhassett Hotel.

Once, while hearing the many stories of Civil War ghosts, a tourist looked down at his feet and found a round of ammunition from the time period. People have had their hair tugged, heard voices whispering in their ears, not to mention many other mischievous encounters with the unknown. Dozens of people who have brought cameras along on the tour have taken photographs of anomalous orbs or smoky images, especially in the Blennerhassett Hotel or the Riverview Cemetery that we travel through. Needless to say, not all haunted tours have actual ghosts and spirits play an active role each evening. This was something that made the Haunted Parkersburg tours unique!

Moundsville Penitentiary

Moundsville is a very serene, rustic place nestled in the mountains of West Virginia's northern panhandle. The people are friendly, the scenery is picturesque, and many of the area's points of interest hold great historical significance. Moundsville was named in honor of the number of Adena burial mounds found in the area. The largest of these mounds is the Grave Creek mound, which is nearly seventy feet tall and 295 feet in diameter. Other points of interest include the Krishna "temple of gold," which was built in the rural parts just outside the city. Visitors can visit the sprawling 2,000-acre complex that has a main temple built from over 200 tons of marble imported from around the world, and encrusted with fourteen-karat gold. People from all over the world come each year to the site to worship or simply out of curiosity.

However, perhaps one of the most intriguing locations to visit in Moundsville also has one of the bloodiest histories of any area in the state. When someone arrives at the Moundsville Penitentiary, he or she cannot help but be awestruck by the sheer beauty and size of the prison. Built in 1876 at a cost of over $300,000 (a very high price in the nineteenth century) thirteen years after West Virginia became a state, the prison was originally designed to house 480 prisoners.

In 1899, the state of West Virginia took control over the execution of prisoners. Before that time, individual counties were responsible for carrying out capital punishment, usually by hanging. The first execution at Moundsville took place in the fall of 1899, shortly after prisoners arrived from all parts of the state. In the fifty years that followed, eighty-five men died on the gallows. In 1951, the electric chair was introduced to Moundsville, but only nine men were put to death in this way between 1951 and 1959. In 1963, West Virginia abolished the death penalty.

Moundsville Penitentiary was way ahead of its time in regard to the education of inmates. The prisoners there were offered some of the first educational facilities of any prison in the country, and they attended class on a regular basis. In addition, each prisoner was given an assigned duty. Some would work in the library, the prison's farm, or even the penitentiary-run coal mine. In the early twentieth century, Moundsville Penitentiary was considered by some

Photograph of the front of Moundsville Penitentiary from the Grave Creek Burial Mound. The construction of Moundsville Penitentiary is similar to Joliet Correctional Facility in Joliet, Illinois.

to be a self-sustaining community behind bars, providing its own food, fuel, and labor from the prison population.

In the early 1930s, Moundsville Penitentiary housed a total of 2,400 prisoners. Although this was temporary due to the prison's decision to add another wing, the overcrowding of the cells was unimaginable. Often the prisoners were over-crowded and many prisoners had no choice but to sleep three to a typical five-by-seven-foot cell. Two prisoners would sleep in the cell bunks, with the third prisoner sleeping on the hard concrete floor. After the construction of North Hall was completed, the prison populace started to dwindle to a more manageable amount of approximately 800 prisoners. The West Virginia Supreme Court declared that the small cell size was a form of cruel and unusual punishment in 1986. By the time the prison closed in 1995, the number had dwindled to approximately 650.

Moundsville Penitentiary has a very violent history. In addition to the executions, it was not uncommon for the morning prison guards to find that at least one of the inmates had committed suicide or was killed during the night. In the early years of the prison, it was not certain how many prisoners died as a result of foul play. Often the death records of the inmates were very vague, often stating simply that a prisoner had died on a certain date. The total number of people murdered at Moundsville will forever remain uncertain, but the death toll is estimated in the hundreds.

New Year's Day, 1986, marked one of the bloodiest days in Moundsville's history. The inmates took control of the prison by taking sixteen correctional officers hostage. The riot began in the prison's cafeteria area. It was later determined to be over poor conditions in the prison living areas and facilities. After days of negotiation, the standoff ended fairly peacefully. None of the hostages were severely injured during the riot, but in the end, three prisoners lost their lives. As a result of the riot, a new cafeteria was built. Ironically, the newest addition to the prison is also reported to be one of the most haunted.

Before delving into details of the paranormal side of the Moundsville Penitentiary, I would like to mention that a warden once received a letter from Charles Manson, who requested to be transferred to Moundsville so he could be closer to McMechen, West Virginia. McMechen is where Manson had spent some of his childhood. Apparently he had some fond memories of the area and wanted to be close to home. Manson has claimed on many occasions that if ever released from his life sentence at Corcoran State Prison in California, he would like to come back to West Virginia to live out the rest of his days. The letter is on display alongside an ornate collection of shanks and the prison's electric chair (that some people still claim has the smell of burnt flesh to this day) in the prison's memorabilia section.

Let the Haunting Begin

A new chapter of the prison's history began shortly after it was shut down in 1995, and most of the prisoners were relocated to Mount Olive Correctional Complex in Mount Olive, West Virginia. The prison was added to the National Register of Historic Places and is still very active today. In addition to hosting a haunted house and a variety of tours, it sponsors an annual mock riot to train law enforcement officers working in prisons from around the country. Rumor has it that two top-grossing films, *The Shawshank Redemption* and *The Green Mile* (both by horror writer Stephen King), were almost filmed at Moundsville.

In recent years, the prison has attracted the attention of the paranormal community and pop culture because of its reputation for being haunted. Moundsville Penitentiary has been the focus of a television reality show, numerous investigations, and a documentary on the hauntings that occur throughout the prison.

In 2000, MTV's *Fear* shot an episode at the penitentiary. Six young people were each asked to perform a series of dares, which ranged from pulling a cloth from an electric chair to staying in a section of the prison reputed to be haunted in complete darkness for fifteen minutes. Each individual who successfully completed the assigned tasks were given $3,000. By the time the show was over, two of the six participants had decided to quit. Each member claimed to have felt a "presence" and at least one claimed to have had contact with the "spirits of the dead" while completing their respective assignments.

Not only has MTV's *Fear* opted to dedicate an episode to Moundsville Penitentiary, but several professional paranormal organizations have conducted full-scale investigations, with some amazing results. Many of these organizations and individuals who have visited the site have not been disappointed. Anomalies ranging from simple orbs to spectral faces have been photographed on these ghost hunts. People have come from as far away as Alabama and New York specifically to take part in the ghost hunt and prison tour.

In the spring of 2001, the prison started to host its own ghost tour. According to the ghost tour's regular guide, tour attendees have numbered in the thousands since its beginning. They want to see where the episode of MTV's *Fear* was filmed and to experience their own paranormal encounters. Between thirty and fifty people show up for each month's haunted tour.

The ghost tour starts at 8:00 P.M. and lasts until 6:00 A.M. the following morning. An official tour of the penitentiary starts off the evening's festivities, followed by the episode of *Fear* that featured the prison. After that, the people on the tour are free to explore the prison at their own risk.

In March of 2002, a paranormal group from Alliance, Ohio, called MAJDA, started to come to the penitentiary for their own ghost hunts. The group is now a fixture of the monthly ghost hunts at Moundsville Penitentiary. In addition to conducting ghost hunts, the group offers their expertise by answering any questions that the tourists may have regarding the hauntings at the prison, or how people can conduct their own paranormal investigations.

Hotspots at Moundsville Prison

Most haunted areas have sections with a higher frequency of paranormal activity. These sections are called "hotspots." Moundsville Penitentiary is no exception. Five areas have been identified as the epicenter of many of the paranormal activity taking place at Moundsville.

People who have no knowledge of the hotspots will often hear voices, see movement in the shadows, or experience other paranormal events while touring the prison. Inevitably, people will claim to experience an overwhelming sensation of hopelessness and dread in certain areas of the prison.

The five areas that have the highest concentration of paranormal activity at Moundsville Penitentiary include Sugar Shack, the Execution Area, North Hall, the maintenance area beneath the Administration Area, and the New Dining Area. Each section is described below with a brief description of what people experience.

Sugar Shack

Sugar Shack was the area where most of the gaming took place, as well as most of the homosexual activity. Many of the guards would not go down into Sugar Shack.

After the prison closed, a group from Ohio came to the Sugar Shack with a Ouija board and other equipment in order to connect with the spirits there. They came up with two names: J. R. and Francis. Later, another group came from Michigan to also attempt communication with spirits. They had no association or affiliation with the group from Ohio. They also brought a Ouija board and came up with the same two names: J. R. and Francis. It is possible that the name Francis could have been a woman's name because Moundsville had women prisoners until 1947.

The following photograph was taken near Sugar Shack on May 24, 2002, by Myssi Gable and Dennis Keefer from Ripley, West Virginia, on their first trip to Moundsville Penitentiary. The photograph was taken in a blackened room and the only light illuminating the area was that of the flash from the disposable camera. One can easily notice the stark profile of an individual facing to the left. Upon closer inspection of the photograph, at least one other face can be discerned. When Myssi and Dennis contacted MAJDA, and sent the group a copy of the photograph, they were surprised to learn that on other occasions, people have photographed faces at the prison.

Execution Area

The Execution Area is also a place where many people have heard and seen things. There were a total of ninety-four people executed here. Undoubtedly many of the "recordings" of the executed, or the actual spirits, still are in this general area. Next to the Administration Area, it has the highest amount of paranormal energy of the entire prison. In the North Yard, the death house has been torn down and replaced with a fenced-in courtyard and basketball court for the prisoners to exercise outside.

Even before being told by the guide about the macabre history of the area, many people who go past the area claim to get a very distinct feeling of hostility, unrest, and uneasiness. People generally say that they have a distinct feeling of sadness and hopelessness when they enter this area. They

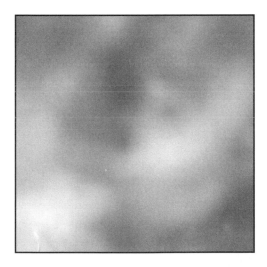

This is an example of the type of photograph that can be taken at Moundsville Penitentiary. Notice the detail of the face and neck of the apparition.

get a similar feeling in other parts of the prison, but by far it is most recognizable in this section of the prison.

This is where a high number of orbs and apparitions tend to get photographed. Moans, sighs, and other sounds are sometimes heard here. It is not uncommon to take a photograph that contains up to as many as thirty to forty orbs. On occasion, tourists will claim to see somebody walking in the shadows, only to find the figure has disappeared into the shadows.

New Dining Area

As a result of the New Year's riot of 1986, this new dining area was built. As with many other parts of the prison, many of the walls still are adorned with the artwork of the prisoners. The entire ambiance of the dining area is one that is almost tangible. Since the prison was closed, people who have walked through the room claimed to hear the sounds of rattling trays and silverware at certain times.

Also, when people enter this area, they sometimes get a distinct feeling of being watched. Although people do experience a great deal of paranormal activity in this area, it is considered one of the weaker hotspots in the prison.

North Hall

Although photographs of an occasional orb or apparition have been taken, the most common type of experience that people have in the North Hall is auditory. It is not uncommon for people to claim to hear cells shutting at times. People who go on the tour often will also hear the distinct sound of metal on metal. In addition, sounds of chains rattling and voices crying have been recorded. Like the Execution Area, a sense of hopelessness and foreboding permeates the entire area.

When asked whether he has had any personal experiences in his area of Moundsville Penitentiary, Mike, a tour guide, stated that he certainly has. "There is a feeling of hopelessness and despair that overwhelms you when you go into North Hall. I've heard moans, sobs, and other sounds. These were usually in the areas of the old Administration Area and the recreation yards in North Hall. Many of the photographs show orbs there. Dan saw something there in the middle of the day."

Dan, another guide who has experienced something in this area of the prison, went to turn off the lights to North Hall one afternoon after the tour. While going through the courtyard of North Hall, he noticed out of the corner of his eye somebody running. He turned to look directly at the person, and saw nobody there. Another person with him confirmed that he also had seen two or three shadows running. After searching in vain for a while, Dan eventually decided that it might be a prisoner's ghost.

Administration Area & Basement: "The Hole"
Although Sugar Shack and the Execution Area are considered hotspots, by far one of the most haunted areas is the Administration Area, directly adjacent to the Execution Area. Along with apparitions and orbs, the occasional discarnate voice, and shadows seen out of the corner of one's eye, the Administration Area has a feature unique to all the other penitentiary hotspots. It is the only area that somebody claimed to have been physically touched by one of the prison's ghosts or spirits.

On one of the tours, while the guide was about to enter the basement of the Administration Building, a girl screamed and said that something touched her on the back of her neck. She was standing by herself and nobody could have touched her. According to the guide, she was obviously frightened; she left the tour immediately after that. After that incident, there was a lot more tension than normal on the rest of the tour.

A prisoner named R. D. Walls was killed here in the 1930s. He was a very quiet man, and apparently on the warden's good side. In exchange for lenient treatment, Walls would offer information about the other prisoners. Soon, the other prisoners discovered that Walls was one of the prime snitches to the warden. They decided to do something about it . . .

One day, while the warden and the maintenance people were taking a smoke break in another section of the prison, the inmates followed Walls down and literally cut him to pieces. His fingers were nearly severed, only hanging to his hands by a small piece of flesh. It took some time for Walls to bleed to death, but his death must have been painful because many of the items used to cut him were dull. They tore, rather than cut, his skin.

After Walls' death, many guards in the guardtower would claim to see a man on the walk above the maintenance area. They would send people to find out who was there, but no one was ever found. One guard eventually came forward and claimed to have recognized the man as R. D. Walls. This didn't seem to surprise either the warden or many of the veteran guards at all. This restless roaming of R. D. Walls continues fairly often to this day.

While conducting an investigation on this section of the prison, I decided to go to the area where Walls' body was found. I walked through the area and thought I heard the woman standing next to me say "Right here" as we entered a doorway leading to the far end of the room. I turned to her and asked what she said. She claimed that she didn't say anything. I decided to take a picture, but my camera wouldn't function. I tried several times, but although the battery indicator showed the batteries were fully charged, the camera simply would not take a picture. After walking through the doorway, the camera worked fine. Other areas of the Administration Area have reportedly been the site of hauntings as well. The maintenance classrooms near the Administration Area were used for either electrical or plumbing classes. The room has not been used for any reason since the prison closed. No one has had a reason to go there. There's no key available to open the lock. The overhead light was mysteriously turned on in an empty, locked room and has been burning solidly ever since.

Many paranormal groups have claimed Moundsville Penitentiary as one of the most haunted sites in West Virginia, and one of the most haunted prisons in the United States. If you are looking for an excellent opportunity to conduct a ghost hunt, this would definitely be worth the trip. For more information on the monthly ghost hunts, please call the prison directly (see Appendix B, page 101).

Continuing Investigations

My role in investigating haunted areas has changed somewhat over the last several years. Instead of simply going to an individual's house, I have found myself actually teaching people how to conduct investigations on their own. When I left for Kentucky after my experiences with Haunted Parkersburg, the demands of ghost hunting full-time were so great that I found myself torn between doing investigations and finishing college. Although I loved helping others solve their paranormal problems, I realized that the ghost hunting would have to be something I did occasionally on the side, while I pursued my career in psychology.

Today, I find myself more of a consultant than an in-the-field ghost hunter; this is a role that I am quite pleased with. I am still current on all of the latest research and theories of the paranormal, but I feel that my path has become that of teaching others to conduct investigations on their own, rather than being in the field full-time.

I receive e-mails and phone calls weekly from people who want advice on what to do about ghosts and spirits in their home, how to effectively perform an investigation, or simply want to share their story with somebody who has experience in the field.

When time permits, I still enjoy going on a ghost hunt in person. I am particularly interested in hauntings that have taken place in older houses, especially those built in the Victorian era or before. I am also fascinated by Civil War apparitions and manifestations. I evaluate the information that an eyewitness shares with me and decide whether or not to investigate a house based on distance from where I live, type of experiences the percipients have had, and many other factors.

Obviously, I cannot investigate every haunting that I am contacted about. However, even if I cannot personally investigate an area, I do reply to as many individual phone calls and e-mails as I can. A network of over fifty ghost hunters (amateur and professional) has been formed in the West Virginia–Ohio-Kentucky area. Instead of personally investigating, I will contact an investigator who lives near the originating report. Usually, a person will investigate the haunting within a week of me contacting them.

Now, I am about to pass on many of those investigation methods to you. This handbook will save you much of the time and hardships that I went through in starting from scratch. One word of advice. Don't feel that you have to adhere to these guidelines to the letter. Over time, as you grow in proficiency, you will develop your own technique, tailor-made to what you feel works for you. Your style may or may not be similar to my style, and that is not a problem. The key to developing your successful style of investigation is to experiment, no matter how unorthodox it may seem. Everyone has his or her style when conducting investigations, but there are two guidelines every good ghost hunter should follow.

1. No matter how you decide to conduct an investigation, don't jump to conclusions. Investigate! In other words, keep your head!

2. Above all, the people you will talk with during your investigations should be given the utmost respect and courtesy. It is very hard for the average person to even consider consulting a paranormal investigator due to the many norms and taboos in our society. They are relying on you, and if you treat your clientele right, they will surely return the favor by telling trusted friends or family of your professionalism.

In the future, I plan to go to various metaphysical and New Age bookstores to conduct workshops on many of the different levels of paranormal phenomena, including discussions of what is included in this book. These would include, but not be limited to, ghosts and spirits, UFOs, and altered states. A website is also in the planning stages where people can put their stories online for others to read, a test to determine your abilities as a ghost hunter (different scenarios would be given and you would write how you would take care of the situation), a referral guide for your local area, as well as an online shop to purchase information packets and starting ghost-hunting kits and other materials that will make your ghost-hunting experiences much more rewarding.

One

GHOSTS, SPIRITS, AND POLTERGEISTS DEFINED

Before investigating hauntings, it would be a good idea to review what exactly is being investigated. Most people tend to place ghosts, spirits, and poltergeists into one broad category. This chapter will go into detail about the differences between the three, and will give you an idea of what kind of haunting you may be investigating. Depending on the type of investigation, the techniques used will vary.

Ghosts and Apparitions

Best described as a form of recording, similar to an audio or videotape, a ghost is the residual energy of a person, animal, or even an inanimate object. There is no life force left; a ghost simply "plays" the same scene over and over. Usually, if a person has performed a repetitious act for a long time, he or she will have left a psychic impression, or "groove," in that area. This groove may stay in the area long after the person has moved or died. Most of the time, the apparitions found at battlefields will be ghosts. Considering the intensity of wartime trauma or skirmishes, a great deal of psychic energy will create a massive groove.

The best way to describe a recording to people who are not familiar with ghosts is to use the following analogy. Imagine driving a large pickup truck on a muddy road. The pickup will leave its tire tracks in the mud, giving the next person who passes an impression of the tread. To the untrained eye, only the fact that a vehicle had passed is obvious. Closer examination by an experienced person can exactly tell the type of tire by the specific pattern it's left in the mud. Through experience and research, the pattern can be traced to the type of truck that uses such a tire.

The tracks will eventually deteriorate (through rain, erosion, and other vehicles driving along the same route) to the point that you would not be able to determine what vehicle made the tracks. Eventually, the tracks will be replaced by more recent tracks. If the truck traveled down the same road day after day, the tracks would be more pronounced than if it only went that route once.

This deterioration principle holds true for ghost recordings, with one exception. Recordings can be "recharged" by a person who has an aura similar to the person who made the recording in the first place. This is why one family can live in a house for years without experiencing anything paranormal, but when another family member moves into the same house, ghostly activity tends to start almost immediately. This is also why some people, upon entering a haunted area, tend to get tired or nauseated. Additionally, people who are very empathic can experience unexplained mood changes. More will be discussed about recharging a haunting later.

Types of Apparitions

All apparitions do not take the form of visual images. Many people tend to think that a ghost or apparition must always be visible; ghosts can be encountered using each of the senses. Usually visual, auditory, tactile, or olfactory apparitions appear in conjunction with each other, but occasionally only one sense is involved. There have been reports of manifestations that have included each of the other senses, particularly the auditory and tactile. Although smells (usually flowers and other natural scents) and sounds (such as church bells or voices) have been reported, they are less common than the visual apparition. Even more rare is a manifestation that involves the sense of taste.

Visual

This is the appearance of a person, animal, or object (yes, animals and inanimate objects can be ghosts as well) that was commonly associated with the area during life. There are varying levels to which a ghost can be seen. Some can be seen in their entirety, as if the recording or ghost was a living, breathing individual. However, most visual apparitions are either hazy or blurry, as if he or she were a bit out of focus. Equally likely, a person seeing an apparition will see a fully formed clear individual with one or more obvious body parts (legs, head, arms, etc.) missing. This last type appears especially in areas where battles or other violent tragedies have taken place.

Auditory

Sounds associated with a ghost recording are actually more common than any other manifestations. Most often, sounds of conversations or footsteps are heard. Other common sounds associated with the auditory manifestations include doors opening and closing, singing and music, yelling, and battle cries. The auditory apparitions are the last to fade away as their recordings also get weaker over time.

Olfactory

This is very similar to the auditory manifestations in the fact that it takes a very long time for the olfactory manifestations to fade away. Usually, everyday odors and scents are connected with the olfactory manifestation. Many hauntings have had an organic scent (most often flowers such as rose or lavender) that occurs just prior to or just after a visual or auditory apparition. Other common scents include food being prepared; bread baking; pipe, cigar, and gun smoke; as well as alcohol or perfume. In the vast majority of cases, the scents are found to be directly associated with the individual or individuals that are responsible for the haunting.

Tactile

There are really two levels of this type of manifestation. The first type occurs in virtually all hauntings. A noticeable change in the room temperature for no apparent reason is one of the common signs that a ghost or spirit is present. Generally, a room gets colder by at least five to twenty degrees Fahrenheit depending on the amount of paranormal activity. Although this is the rule, there have been exceptions—hauntings in which the room temperature actually increases significantly. When there is a noticeable rise in temperature, typically the haunting is caused by a fire in which one or more individuals perished.

The second type of tactile manifestation occurs when an individual can actually feel the recording. A brush of the hair, a gentle breeze, and a scratch are all examples of a tactile manifestation. Of the four types of manifestations discussed, tactile manifestations occur least frequently. However, when it does present itself, this type of tactile manifestation is usually very slight. Examples of a tactile manifestation include feeling a slight wind in a closed-off room or a slight tug on a person's clothing with nobody in the immediate vicinity.

Spirits

Most people are of the opinion that the terms "ghost" and "spirit" can be used interchangeably. This is definitely not the case. While a ghost is simply a psychic recording or groove, a spirit is the actual sentient presence, or soul, of an individual or individuals who have remained in the material world after his or her physical body has died. I strongly believe that if somebody can help a spirit that is trapped in this world move to the afterlife, he or she has an obligation to do so. This section will describe the reasons that spirits haunt an area, discuss ways that spirits and the living can communicate with one another, and then finally go into detail about how to help the spirit move to the afterlife.

Types of Spirits

There are four main reasons a person's spirit stays behind after death.

One, the spirit does not realize his or her own death. Sometimes, if a person dies suddenly or very violently, he or she may not actually realize that death has occurred. This would obviously be very confusing and difficult for the person who has passed on. Naturally, he or she would make many attempts to contact their living loved ones, usually with little or no success.

Only if a spirit is convinced that he or she is no longer living will the haunting cease. There are a few ways to help convince the spirit of this. In each case, the main step is to determine where the spirit spends most of its time, or in other words, the locations it is haunting. Once this is found, there are a few options. First, you can simply talk aloud to the spirit, telling the spirit that it has died and that it is time to move on for its sake as well as for its loved ones. A second way is to simply project very strong thoughts and feelings to the spirit, telling it to move on. This may appear similar to the first technique, but in actuality the mental projection is somewhat more reliable than the verbal technique because the thoughts are projected directly toward the spirit. A third technique is to bring in a channeler or spirit-releasement guide to attempt a spirit-releasement session. This final technique will be discussed in detail later.

It may take a series of attempts of verbal or mental communication directed to the spirit before it begins to comprehend what is being said. Just as many apparitions may appear fuzzy or out-of-focus to us, we tend to have the same appearance to the spirit. This is because the veil between the spirit and material world often prevents us from clearly communicating with the dead. The veil between the two realms is the thinnest, and communication is most effective, on occasions of special anniversaries or dates of importance.

Even if a person is not attempting communication to a spirit, the spirit may eventually realize it is dead gradually by simply putting the pieces together logically. People act differently, ignoring the spirit, and many aspects of their loved one's lives may gradually change. A perfect example of a spirit finally acknowledging his own death is the role of Bruce Willis' character in *The Sixth Sense*. Only after a series of events does he acknowledge his own death, allowing him and his wife to move on.

The second reason is the spirit has unfinished business in the material world. Death can come at the most unexpected time in our lives. People generally have an idea of what they want to accomplish before they die, but sometimes they are not given an opportunity to bring closure to their important business. A person may have an unfinished project or want to make certain that a loved one is well taken care of. This desire to complete business may be enough to keep a person who has died in spirit form tied to the physical world.

A spirit can haunt an area for as long as the promise is unkept, or as long as the project is unfinished. This can become very problematic for individuals who happen to be in the vicinity of the haunting and have no idea of what the project or promise may be. If the spirit attempts communication with no success, the hauntings may become more intense, often to the point of physical movement and other manifestations that could frighten, or even harm, the eye-witnesses to the haunting.

There are two ways that a spirit, bound by an unkept promise or unfinished project, can be helped to the afterlife. The first way is to find out what the promise or project was, and then help the spirit accomplish its fulfillment. Perhaps the easiest way to discover this is to bring in a spirit-release guide, medium, or channeler to communicate with the spirit. They should ask the spirit what keeps it earthbound, and what would fulfill the promise. Pay close attention to what is relayed because leaving out a simple step in the procedure may keep the spirit from dissipating. A variation of this method that does not involve a channeler or guide is to do some detective work, find out who the possible spirit is, and use any information you find about that person to deduce what the promise or project may have been. In some cases, simply acknowledging the spirit and bringing its plight out in the open may be just enough to help it move on.

The second way that you can help this type of spirit is to convince the spirit that the promise or business is not as important as moving on. Depending on how dedicated the person was to the project or promises, this may be a difficult task. If you can use the channeler or guide to explain to the spirit that its presence in this world is possibly unhealthy for remaining loved ones, it will be more inclined to let go and travel to the afterlife.

There is a variation of this type of reasoning. In the case of murder, the spirit may be trapped in the physical world until either the murderer is brought to justice or dies. At that time, the spirit should be released from the confines of the material world and allowed to move on to the afterlife. There is a case in West Virginia history known as "the Greenbrier Ghost."

Elva Zona Heaster died at the hands of her husband, Edward Shue, in 1897. Edward was very strong and aggressive, had previous run-ins with the law, and bragged about his mistreatment of previous two wives, one of whom also died. Elva was married to Edward for approximately two months before her death. Edward was not suspected of killing Elva, until Elva's mother reported seeing her daughter's ghost on four occasions. On each occasion, Elva's spirit explained that Edward had broken her neck. After pleading with the local authorities, Elva's mother had her daughter's body exhumed, and an autopsy was performed. It was found that her neck had indeed been broken. Edward was brought to trial.

Elva's mother was allowed to bring the testimony of her daughter's apparition to the stands, and through that and

The gravesite of Zona Heaster Shue, the Greenbrier Ghost. This is the only account in United States history where a ghost has played a significant role in bringing a murderer to justice.

other evidence that was found against Edward, he was convicted of Elva's murder. Elva's spirit has not been seen since. To this day, the Greenbrier Ghost is the only court case in United States history that has allowed the testimony of a spirit to be considered in the trial and conviction of an alleged murderer.

In the third reason, the spirit wishes to say goodbye before moving on to the afterlife. This is the most common and usually the shortest in duration of all spirit encounters. When people have very close binds to others in life, it is a natural reflex to say goodbye when death approaches. Sometimes a person may die before he or she gets a chance to bid farewell to loved ones. In this case, within a very short time of death his or her spirit may make a brief appearance to let others know of his or her passing.

The people chosen are generally those who have very open minds to the paranormal, who were especially close to the deceased, or were unable to visit the dying person before death. The spirit relays a message that he or she is all right, on the way to a better place, and that the loved ones should not worry. Generally, a spirit will visit only one or two people before moving on. In the case of accidents or sudden deaths, people hundreds of miles away may sense a loved one's death within seconds of its occurrence.

Most of the time, the spirit visits a loved one while he or she is asleep. However, visitations during the waking hours are not uncommon under special circumstances. There is no reason to attempt to help these spirits move on to the afterlife. Very rarely is a haunting caused by a spirit that is saying goodbye to a loved one; the spirit is simply making a small courtesy visit before making a much longer journey to the spirit realm.

The last reason is when the spirit wishes to offer guidance to a special loved one. The fourth type of spiritual visitation is actually a variation of the third. This type of spiritual visitation can appear to a loved one going through some very difficult situation or stage in his or her life. Again, the visitation usually makes an appearance in dream form, many years after the individual has died, but offers insight to the dreamer about the presenting problem. After the information is passed and encouragement is given, the spirit visitation generally ends.

This type of visitation could be dismissed as a simple dream if it were not for a few factors. First, in this type of visit, information is sometimes conveyed to the dreamer that he or she would have no knowledge of otherwise. Information such as the location of important documents, the names of the deceased's friends that should be contacted, or many other things can be conveyed to the sleeper by the spirit. When the person that was visited follows up on these tips, the information generally turns out to be accurate. Second, a familiar scent is usually present and is strong enough to wake the dreamer and anybody in close proximity. Cigar smoke, perfume, and other personal scents associated with the deceased are very noticeable in the air, and can linger for many minutes.

A guidance visitation does not necessarily need to be only about specific information to help out a loved one. Many visitations by spirits can actually offer a glimpse into the future challenges or crossroads in a person's life.

Lucy, an old colleague of mine, had a dream in which her grandfather visited her at a very transitional time in her life, to offer guidance. When she was fourteen, Lucy's grandfather died of throat cancer. The two were very close and Lucy was devastated by his death. She had the dream when she was twenty-years old, but now, nearly ten years after the dream has taken place, Lucy is beginning to find out exactly how accurate her grandfather's message really was. Here is her personal account.

My mom, dad, brother, and I were at "Mom-Mom's" house visiting my uncle, aunt, and two cousins who were in from out-of-town. Mom-Mom was busy preparing a meal while the rest of us were helping out and socializing. I decided to venture upstairs where I found "Granddaddy" waiting for me. He said, "I need to show you something." He led me into the upstairs half-bathroom and shut the door. Immediately behind that door, in the corner of the room, was a door that does not physically exist in the house itself. He opened the door, which housed a drafting table with a very large pad of graphing paper. There were protractors and measuring devices of all kinds hanging from and lying on the shelf above. He took a silver-leaded pencil and made a dot. He said, "Lucy, right now you are here. You are going to go here, here, and here (making three new dots in an arched pattern on the paper), and when you get here, you will find true happiness." I just looked on rather dumbfounded, not knowing what to say or do at that time. He then said that he had to go. I insisted that he stay, but he advised that he could not. He faded so that I could see the paneling on the wall through him. He then turned into a silver dot and flew away.

Lucy felt very strongly that her grandfather visited her in a dream that night. She said, "This memory afforded me the strength and conviction to get on the path that felt . . . conducive for my future happiness in life." Since this visitation,

Lucy has discovered the meaning of two of the four stars. The first dot was a very traumatic car accident in which she could have been killed, but walked away with only very minor injuries. The second dot was the birth of her son, which has changed her life for the better. It helped her realize the importance of personal responsibility and others' complete reliance on her. The third star represented her growing spirituality, which coincided with her return to college. The fourth star has yet to manifest in Lucy's life at this time, but she feels that the fourth crossroads will take place within four or five years.

Spirit Communication

Spirits, unlike ghosts, can occasionally communicate with the living. Usually, if a person frequents a place where the deceased spent much of his or her time, or where he or she died, a form of psychic communication can result. Rather than outright verbal communication, a spirit usually communicates on a much more subtle level.

A particularly sensitive person can pick up on the mood of a spirit. Sudden and unexplained feelings of sadness or melancholy are common indications, especially if encountered in only one room or area. Have you ever entered a room just after some people have been fighting and noticed a tension in the air? This is the same principle with picking up on spirits, although the spiritual tension can last much longer and can be more pronounced.

Most often, the living will have no acknowledgment of the spirits' attempts at contact. Usually, contact is finally made in the hypnogogic state, which the half-waking, half-sleeping beta state. In hypnosis, the hypnogogic state is achieved to get to the person's subconscious to achieve effective results. In this state, people tend to be more open to suggestion, are much more aware of their surroundings, and are able to receive more psychic impressions, including attempts at contact from the spirit world.

Animals and small children are especially aware of paranormal activity, usually even before adults who are sensitive to such phenomena. A pet may suddenly become very alert and, depending on the type of spirit or ghost, may either become very friendly or very apprehensive about it. Usually children under five years of age are also very sensitive to ghosts and spirits. In many cases, they have "imaginary friends" that may have been alive at one time. I personally know of a three-year-old who had an imaginary friend with large glasses, stubble, and a very specific scar on his forehead. Later it was found that someone who had died in their house over forty years before had those exact same characteristics. The child eventually said that the man "went away home" after a medium had spiritually cleansed the house. The child was at daycare at the time, and unaware of the medium visiting the house.

Spirit Releasement and Dream Communication

For hundreds of years, people have claimed to have the special ability to contact the spirits of the dead. The spiritualist movement reached its peak in the Victorian era, during which séances and attempts to contact the spirit world were an everyday occurrence. Granted most of the séances, and channelers associated with them, were staged, but many people were convinced that contact was being made with the spirits of loved ones. Although most were hoaxes, some honest channelers worked with the sole intent of helping the spirits to "break on through to the other side."

Today, there are still people who are particularly in tune with spiritual contact and put their skills to practical use by helping the spirit move from a haunted area. These individuals are called "spirit-release guides." The spirit-release guide usually works alongside a channeler to make contact with the spirit. Their purpose is to help the spirit move into the light in order to prepare for the next life. Naturally, there is usually some form of resistance because the spirits may not want to believe that they are actually dead, do not want to leave their loved ones, or do not wish to leave the world without finishing some important business or keeping a special promise. The spirit-release guide actually helps the spirits accept their deaths and work through any issues that may be keeping them earthbound. Once a spirit has accepted the assistance of a spirit-release guide, the transition is usually very smooth.

Another way that a spirit can communicate with the living is through dreams. This usually takes place during one of two cases. First, just after the person has died, he or she will visit one or two loved ones to bid them farewell and to assure them that he or she is all right. The second case takes place when somebody has been having some very difficult problems and the loved one's spirit can come back to offer reassurance and, in some cases, guidance. Visitation dreams are generally much more vivid and realistic than normal dreams. They also tend to bring a sense of peace and serenity to the dreamer. In a few cases, the dreamer can notice a familiar scent associated with the spirit while he or she was alive. Pipe tobacco, perfume, etc., are commonly described when somebody tells of a visitation.

Poltergeists

The third type of paranormal event that ghost hunters can encounter is the *poltergeist* (German for "noisy ghost"). At first glance, the poltergeist may appear similar to ghosts and spirits, but upon closer examination, the differences far outweigh the similarities.

One characteristic in which poltergeists differ from ghosts and spirits is that the activity is usually concentrated around one person, rather than an area. This person is called the "epicenter." If the epicenter gets irate at the poltergeist and demands that the activity ceases, generally there is an abrupt stop in any activity for awhile.

There are some common traits among most epicenters. It has been found that poltergeists tend to manifest around individuals who are dealing with great physical and emotional stress, and that most are adolescents going through puberty. Another common characteristic is that epicenters are fairly quiet-natured people, without a great many friends or associates. They tend to spend most of their time alone and are of average to above-average intelligence. Epicenters are not really prone to playing practical jokes or pranks, which makes the poltergeist a very unexpected event.

Many paranormal investigators believe that poltergeists tend to manifest around individuals who have been psychologically suppressed and injured in some way. These psychological injuries could include, but are not limited to, neglect, physical and mental abuse, and sexual molestation. In an environment where this is commonplace, pleas can go ignored and unnoticed for a long time. Thus, the epicenter cannot find a way to voice his or her aggression and begins to hold emotions inside, constantly building them upon one another.

After the emotions have welled up as much as the epi-center can take, there is a breaking point in which the person subconsciously lashes out to release the pressure. This lashing-out of emotion is so concentrated that a poltergeist can form. That could explain why only one person is gener-ally chosen as an epicenter.

This apparent intelligence would add credence to the idea that the poltergeists are actually a form of spirit. Knocking and rappings are very common in poltergeist hauntings. These sounds can emanate from almost any kind of solid surface, such as walls, beds, floors, or tables. There is at first no discernible pattern to the knocks and raps. If the polter-geist persists for any length of time, a primitive form of communication may develop. The epicenter can ask a pol-tergeist a question and different sequences of knocks and raps can represent different answers. This works best with simple yes or no questions, or with answers that have numerical value. The sounds of rappings that have been reported with the poltergeist tend to be of the same nature that is often heard at séances, which is a hollow, metallic sound.

Perhaps the most common phenomenon associated with the poltergeist is the movement of objects. When poltergeist activity begins, the misplaced objects are simply found in odd places where they would not normally be found. For example, small objects such as keys or eyeglasses can be found in the freezer or above a cabinet. If the poltergeist con-tinues to become stronger, the movements will also grow more intense as well.

Furniture and appliances may be moved in a moment without any warning. Light bulbs may be unscrewed while the lamp is turned on. At the beginning stage, there is no direct contact with the epicenter or other family members, but moving furniture, stacked dishes, or overturned appliances can be unnerving to the typical family.

In the more advanced stages of poltergeist activity, the objects actually can be thrown at the epicenter or other people. These attacks are uncommon and only happen in the most sinister and powerful poltergeist accounts. Some psychologists believe that this takes place because of an unconscious wish on the part of the epicenter to harm him- or herself.

There is one bit of good news for the family that becomes involved with a poltergeist. The average duration for a poltergeist outbreak is between three weeks and two years. Over time, most poltergeist activity diminishes and disappears completely, with no sign or recurrence.

When investigating hauntings, pay particular attention to the family's lifestyle as well as the age of the epicenter. After a few encounters, you may notice a distinct pattern in the personality traits of the epicenter of these events, which will definitely help in your future investigations with poltergeists.

Entities

Entities are what many people would consider angels or demons. They are completely spiritual or ethereal in nature and actually have never lived as human beings. This type of manifestation is fairly uncommon and in the vast majority of cases where entities are suspected, the real culprits turn out to be simply ghosts or spirits.

Entities will act differently than spirits, ghosts, or poltergeists. Remember that ghosts are simply recordings that have no way of communicating with the living. There is simply no life left. Spirits may actually communicate with people, but usually tend to do so by thought, dreams, or by signs that may be of special significance to a loved one or the people toward whom the message is directed. As for the poltergeist, although there may appear to be a slight intelligence involved, the actions are generally centered around one individual.

One of the major characteristics that may clue you in on the fact that you are dealing with an entity is an overwhelming sense of good or evil associated with the apparition. Dealing with entities is definitely one case where listening to your feelings and instincts may be the best thing you can do. There are two major types of entities that a ghost hunter may encounter: angelic entities and demonic entities.

Angelic Entities

Angelic entities serve mainly as messengers or protectors. Generally, when an angelic entity is encountered, it is a very private matter between the entity and the individual or individuals that were meant to witness it. Other people in the room or area may not actually see the angelic entity, but they may feel a very strong sense of peace and well-being. Apparitions of Jesus Christ and the Virgin Mary would be included in this category.

Angels are most often encountered during the near-death experience, or at a time of extreme stress for the person(s) being visited. After such a visitation, the person may actually have a complete lifestyle change, often putting aside old habits and dedicating their lives to making others aware of the goodness associated with God and the universe.

Encountering Demonic Entities

Demonic entities are not very common, but chances are that if you stay in the ghost-hunting profession long enough, you may very well encounter one or two cases that involve a demon. Demons are usually encountered only after an individual or individuals invite one into their lives in one fashion or another. The most common way is for people to play with various forms of divination that they have not been trained in properly, or even at all. The typical scene, where a group of teenagers at a slumber party pull out a Ouija board, is a perfect example of inviting a demonic presence into their lives.

A person who is not well versed in the occult may play with the Ouija board in order to find an answer to an everyday problem or question. "Who will I marry?" "What will I be like when I grow up?" "Is there anybody out there who can hear me?"

If two or more people are using the Ouija board, the entity will usually concentrate on the one with the lowest psyche. In this case, psyche refers to the amount of natural or learned spiritual protection a person may have. A person's psyche is like any other ability in that it can vary from person to person, but it can be strengthened through study, practice, and discipline.

This type of entity may answer one or two questions in order to lull those using the Ouija board into false sense of trust. The demon generally appears in the guise of a sympathetic spirit that just wants to help. The more a person uses the Ouija board, the more likely the entity can come to this realm to wreak havoc.

Another way that a demon can unwittingly be introduced into the home of a individual or individuals is through automatic writing. Although automatic writing can be a very useful tool to access the subconscious and some of the higher spiritual realms, without the proper precautions, it can be a homing beacon for a demonic entity. Once an entity of this type arrives, it is very difficult to send it back to its original plane of existence. Under no circumstances should a ghost hunter attempt to work on an investigation that may have a demonic entity present. A priest or other professional versed in dealing in this type of phenomena should be consulted.

Recharging a Haunting

Over time, the "groove," or ghost, will get weaker, and will eventually disappear entirely. However, hauntings can be recharged under the right circumstances, especially in any area where there is a great amount of energy transference. If a sentimental object of the dead person is brought into the area, the apparitions can be recharged. However, there are a few other reasons that may cause a ghost recording to be recharged. These circumstances involve aura similarities, renovations, large electrical fields, and séances or Ouija boards.

Aura Similarities

It is common knowledge in parapsychology and metaphysics that every living thing has a life force, or aura. In

Biblical times, this was often referred to as a "halo." According to many experts in the metaphysical community, the aura is the life essence or psychic field that makes each of us unique. The aura of a living individual may be very similar to that of the person who has left the ghost recording or spirit. Considering how similar the aura field is, the recording or spirit may actually borrow some of this energy from the person. This makes the ghost or spirit stronger while leaving the person feeling very fatigued and drained for hours. The energy level of the person will eventually be renewed given time and rest.

Renovations to a Physical Place

Renovations to a room or building may also cause an increase in ghost and spirit activity. When additions to a house or building change the overall appearance of the layout of the house, paranormal activity usually is concentrated in the area of the renovations. Most likely, the apparitions are visual or auditory, although in some cases there have been reports of "missing" items, such as tools.

In the case of an earthbound spirit that is attempting to communicate, its efforts may be redoubled by any major changes to its surroundings. This is especially the case if the renovations have something to do with an unkept promise. For example, if a person promised to keep a family house in good repair and that place is being demolished to build something else, the appearance of the spirit may increase dramatically, and do as much as possible to prevent the new house from being completed.

Large Electrical Fields or Disturbances

Large electrical disturbances or fields can also "recharge" a ghost recording. Places near electrical towers have often had an increased amount of paranormal activity in general. Not only are ghosts and spirits more prevalent, but other paranormal events, such as UFOs, are also more common. The theory is that it is drawing energy from the large electrical source in much the same way that the ghost drains energy from the aura. If there are increased electrical disturbances in a house, such as light bulbs blowing out at an increased rate, a large number of fuses blowing, etc., there is a chance that the cause could be a ghost. (Before making this conclusion, make certain that the electrical wiring in an area is sound.)

Séances or Ouija Boards

As many people do not know that there is a difference between a spirit and a ghost, they may attempt to contact a ghost in any way possible. The most common method is through a séance or Ouija board. Any organized attempt to conjure or contact spirits of the dead in this manner will generally bring about many unexpected results. In the case of a ghost, the energy used to "contact" it could be used to recharge it, making the appearances more frequent. In the case of a spirit, you may be getting much more than bargained for.

At this point, I would like to offer one word of caution about attempting to contact spirits in this fashion. You may be opening a vortex or doorway for malevolent spirits instead of the ones you were originally attempting to contact. This is especially dangerous with people who do not know exactly what they are doing in regards to séances and Ouija boards. I would highly recommend to anyone investigating a haunting not to use these forms of communication, or get involved in any investigation in which the eyewitnesses used either.

Two

RESEARCHING A SUSPECTED HAUNTED AREA

In addition to knowing how to identify various types of phenomena, it is important to know how to conduct an investigation. A great deal of the haunting's investigation takes place before you even enter the haunted area.

There are many ways to investigate a haunted house, but they all begin with research. Keep in mind that there will be a lot of historical research necessary to accurately investigate the haunting and to help those living in the haunted area understand the nature of the manifestations.

There is a very important procedure to adhere to when conducting an effective investigation, involving at least four main phases: (1) conduct an initial interview of any eyewitnesses to the event. Firsthand accounts are very important to a ghost hunter and should be taken seriously and documented accurately; (2) visit the local library, courthouse, or other locations for information independent of the eyewitness accounts. Researching independent sources is the key to this phase; a good investigator wants to be as unbiased as possible; (3) return to the scene of the haunting to interview the witnesses about any recent paranormal activity (since the initial interview), and to actually search the area for any signs of ghostly activity. At this point, the investigators should use their equipment (see step three, page 33); and lastly, (4) make a determination and conclusion based on all of your collected data. The following is a much more detailed description of each phase of an investigation, but first a few words of caution.

Be Cautious, not Gullible

People contact paranormal investigators for a number of reasons. Most calls for a ghost hunter can fall into one of the following categories. Learning to distinguish which category a person falls into is one of the most important skills you can learn in this field: (1) Most people are in need of legitimate assistance and do not know where else to go with their paranormal problems; (2) others simply need to have an understanding person in this field to reassure them that these events can and do happen; (3) however, there are some people who are looking to have fun at the investigator's expense. They may contact you or a member of your group and share an "encounter" that is nothing short of fantastic. These are often young people out for a prank; (4) some are interested in making a name for themselves by fabricating an elaborate hoax. Finding a paranormal investigator to substantiate and validate their claims can only add credence to their story; and (5) some mentally ill individuals may contact you to help them.

When talking to somebody initially on the phone, take the person's name, address, phone number and other pertinent information (including the best time to meet or call back), the location of the haunting, and how often it takes place and the particulars of the event (who, what, when, where, how). Then tell the person that it may be a day or so before you can return the person's call to arrange an initial investigation.

Take into account voice inflections, personality, etc. Do not agree to meet the person on the initial phone call. Of course, there are exceptions to each of these rules, but most of all, use your judgment.

Phase 1: Interview Eyewitnesses

If you are conducting an independent investigation, it would be prudent to contact the people living in the haunted house to arrange an interview, if they choose to comply. Be very friendly and professional. If they decide not to work with you, respect their wishes. This section is for those who have either contacted you initially or have agreed to talk with you about their haunted house. After gathering the basic information, make certain to get the names of previous tenants, if possible. (You can contact them at a later time to see if they have had any encounters, too.)

Sometimes people will be very hesitant about telling anybody, especially strangers, about any paranormal encounters they are experiencing. Assurance of the confidential nature of the information will usually lead to cooperation. Confidentiality is a must!

It is also very important to record information regarding family history, which can be just as important as the house history. "Did any of your parents/grandparents ever have anything like this happen?" or "Do you sometimes dream of things before they happen?" Check in the appendix for a questionnaire to use when interviewing witnesses (see page 93).

Answer your interviewees' questions honestly and to the best of your ability. A good balance is always preferred; instead of simply taking information from the family, offer some answers as well. Talk with the family; be conversational, but also professional. After all, they are your investigation's main source of the information on ghosts and spirits!

At the end of the first interview, you can arrange another meeting with the haunted house's residents. Go over what the eyewitnesses experienced and write down any details you feel are important to the investigation. Share with the residents information about the house's history. If you find any newspaper clippings about the area while doing research at the library, offer a photocopy to the homeowners or tenants. Again, at all times, be courteous and sincere. Always keep in touch with the witnesses of any information you find.

Body Language

Body language is quite possibly the single most important factor to take into account when interviewing an eyewitness. Many people have the verbal ability to exaggerate, or outright lie, but most tend to overlook the revealing nature of their body language.

Body language can convey a myriad of information about the subject's truthfulness, whether he or she is concealing information, fabricating something, and many other things. There are many books on the subject that would be very helpful if you want to pursue the topic on more than a basic level. Although I would not suggest relying solely on body language as an indicator of somebody telling you the truth, keep in mind that although most people who are deceptive toward you may have practiced the spoken account, rarely do they practice their body language. There are many books on the subject available. This ghost hunters' guide cannot contain all of the subtleties involved in reading body language. However, listed below are some of the more common cues to look for when interviewing an eyewitness.

Eye Contact

If a person shifts his gaze from side-to-side, and never makes eye contact, there is a chance that he's not telling the truth. Conversely, if the individual is staring directly into your eyes, be cautious as well. Generally, a person telling the truth will have a moderate amount of eye contact.

Crossing Arms and Legs

When a person sits across from you with his or her arms and legs crossed, it is generally construed as a sign of defensiveness. Either he does not believe what you are telling him, doesn't wish to share information, or may be uncomfortable with the situation.

Moving Posture Frequently

If the person shifts his or her position more than three times a minute, he or she may be lying to you. The shifting is generally done as an unconscious distraction and gives the person a very brief opportunity to think about how he or she is going to answer your question.

Leaning

If an individual leans toward the interviewer, that is an indication that he or she is interested in the conversation. Usually this indicates a strong willingness to cooperate. However, if he or she leans away from the interviewer, that person is not being receptive to the question or topic of conversation. A greater chance of defensiveness will likely be encountered in this case.

Phase 2: Get Independent Information

Once you get the information from the family (including witnesses' names and places or dates of specific events), you should continue to the next step of the investigation by gathering as much independent data as possible from the leads you received. Generally, this means going to the local library to gather as much information about it as you can. Who built the house? Was it in a residential or business location? Was it near a cemetery or battlefield? In the appendix (see page 97), you will find a list of questions to ask when conducting research on a haunted area. Most medium to large libraries have a section on, or archive of, local history. Depending on the intensity of a haunting, expect to spend at least a few days or weeks conducting research pertaining to your leads.

When you do this research, make sure to bring a notebook, pen, and lots of change for the photocopier. (Many libraries that do have archives do not allow their books, newspapers, and other records to leave the building.) The library archives will have available town records, newspaper clippings, and other information. It will take a bit of work, but the more information you have, the better prepared you will be when you go to the place in question. The library is one of your most valuable tools.

By conducting research in this manner, you will probably find some amazing facts about the haunted area. In addition, you will learn a great deal about the history of the town, which can prove valuable when interviewing people. It is very important to remember that, to be a good ghost hunter, you also need to be a good historian.

In addition to the library, you may need to go to the local courthouse, which should have topographical maps of the area. Photocopy or otherwise obtain a copy of the map, if possible. If this is not permitted, simply photograph or copy freehand the section of map you need.

Once you have some historical facts, it is time to talk with people who may have a great amount of factual information about the area, or even the legends behind it. Residents of retirement communities and nursing homes are valuable resources, and often overlooked. They will be very happy to share stories and accounts they personally experienced, or have been told about when they were younger. They may even know the identity of the spirit or ghost.

You could also place an announcement on the community or home's bulletin board asking for any information. Every time I did this during an investigation, I always received at least one or two phone calls from people who helped me immensely. One retired person was so impressed with the work I was doing that he came along on an investigation. He helped by telling me about the architecture, the history of the location, and other facts that I would have never found simply by reading a newspaper archive.

Phase 3: Investigating the Haunted Area

There are seven specific steps to effectively investigate the haunted area itself. Each step is vital to having an accurate and successful paranormal investigation, so it is imperative that they are followed very closely. The more thorough a job you do with your investigation, the more likely you will be able to find useable information and data for your ghost hunt.

Step One: Determine time necessary to do an investigation

The length of time to spend on an investigation varies from place to place. Take into account the frequency of paranormal activity, size of the house, and the amount of direct access you have to the haunted area. A good standard is to allow 30–60 minutes per room. Dedicate more time to rooms with more activity. This should be plenty of time to take photographs, record for voices, take temperature readings, and other tests to detect paranormal activity. Determine beforehand how much time you need and discuss it with any people directly involved in the haunting.

One hotel that I investigated for the Haunted Parkersburg tours would only allow me to investigate between 10:00 P.M. and 8:00 A.M. The equipment and investigation might have had a negative impact on their business. I obliged not only out of respect, but the night auditor was more than accommodating to share her accounts. I soon found that most of the paranormal activity took place between those hours anyway!

Step Two: Tour the Area

Familiarize yourself with the area you are investigating, possibly with the owners or residents to have them pinpoint where any activity has taken place. Photograph the front of the area to use as a reference. If there are any other eyewitnesses, ask them to show you where the paranormal activity took place and mark it on your map. Be sure to take clear notes of what the eyewitnesses say. If possible, use your microcassette recorder to record the conversation.

While touring the area, be observant of any peculiarities that may be partially or entirely responsible for some of the manifestations. Ask yourself while touring the rooms: Are the doors balanced, or do they swing by themselves due to structural problems? Are there any apparent drafts by the windows that could cause movement or create a draft? Could there be any pipes that may cause knocking sounds?

Step Three: Setting Up and Using Your Ghost-Hunting Equipment

Always test the equipment before placing it. Make certain that there are fresh batteries, cassettes, and film inserted before beginning an investigation. Concentrate your efforts on the rooms that have the most activity.

Always document the condition of each piece of equipment immediately prior to using your equipment and again once you are packing them away. Take note if there was any tampering of the equipment. When you are finished with the room, pick up your equipment and continue to each room until you are finished. Have a separate cassette for each room if possible. This way, you can pick up a particular cassette to review it without spending time cueing the tape to the section you want. Also, if you keep the tapes separate for each room, you will have no chance of accidentally erasing anything important on the tapes. Listen to the tapes after the tour of the area, and if you find nothing on the tapes, simply reuse them.

Step Four: Writing Down Impressions

Not only should you document the readings from the equipment, also take notice of anything observed by you, other members of the group, or any eyewitnesses who accompany you. Always have a pad of paper and pen handy to write down even the briefest of ideas that come to mind. It may seem insignificant at the time, but even the smallest clue can make a difference in an investigation. Write down any and all impressions, readings, changes, etc., that you experience, as it will be difficult to distinguish between what is important and what is not at this time.

Step Five: Organizing and Searching for Anything Anomalous

When the tour of the area is concluded, return to your base of operations to organize data and to look for anything anomalous on film or tape. Compare notes of personal accounts you received from personal eyewitnesses. If you have anything anomalous on film or tape, put that piece aside and allow other group members examine it. Discuss the findings and develop a conclusion.

Step Six: Determine if you need to make another visit

If you feel that a return trip to the haunted area is needed, contact the owners or residents and complete steps one through five again until you have gathered all necessary information. You may have to repeat the steps many times to get all the information you need to make a decision. With each subsequent visit, be as observant as you were when you initially investigated the area. Never take anything for granted, or overlook even the smallest thing that could be useful later. Finally, if it is determined that you do not need to go back to the area, move on to Phase Four (see next page).

Step Seven: Follow All Leads

Researching anything, be it a paranomral investigtion or a thesis for doctorate, is very much like putting together the pieces of a jigsaw puzzle. You know that the information you've gathered is connected, but you don't know how they may fit together until much further into the research process.

A good investigator and researcher will carefully document and categorize all information that he or she finds. Names and numbers of contacts you have talked with are crucial. As I mentioned in the chapter on the ghost-hunting kit, an address book dedicated to your paranormal contacts carried on your person at all times will become one of the investigator's most cherished tools. You can have the information of all the people you met during an investigation at a glance. During the interview, simply fill in their name, address, phone number, and which investigation you interviewed them for.

When you gather new information, follow up on it as soon as possible. This way it is still fresh in your mind. The longer you wait to follow up on a lead, the more likely you will forget part of it, even if you take notes. Preferably, the information should be followed up during the same day, but that cannot realistically be the case in every investigation. I always follow up on any information or leads within one or two days at the latest.

Following up on a lead is more detailed that simply researching documentation and interviewing people. Accurate documentation is crucial for an accurate and productive investigation. I write a summary of each day's events. I gather all of my notes, contact information, photographs, instrument readings, recordings, etc. that were used during the day and document what I have into the computer. The format that I use to summarize the day's events is as follows: (1) First, I start a new word-processing document (Microsoft Word or Word Perfect, for example) and enter the current date in the upper left corner; (2) I briefly summarize the events that transpired during the day. This should only be a few sentences because more detailed information will follow; and (3) I dedicate a section for the names, addresses, and phone numbers of anyone I spoke with.

Phase 4: Concluding the Investigation

Once you have conducted as much research as possible on a haunting, the final step is to bring the investigation to a close. This phase consists of three basic steps.

Step One: Reaching a Conclusion

Discuss with the other group members to determine the type of haunting you have investigated (ghost, spirit, poltergeist, other paranormal phenomenon, or hoax) and write a summary of your findings. This summary should consist of basic facts, names, places, and reasons that led you to your conclusion. Depending on the intensity of the haunting, the summary may be anywhere from a few paragraphs to several pages.

Step Two: Filing the Information

File away any information and materials in a clearly marked file folder. It would be helpful if the label included the date the investigation began and ended as well as an identifier that you can easily recognize (name, place, etc.). The file should include photographs, negatives, cassette tapes, notes, blueprints, maps, etc.

Step Three: Informing People Involved

Contact the people involved in the haunting and inform them of your conclusion. Again, depending on the nature of the investigation and the rapport developed with them, this contact may be in the form of a phone call, e-mail, letter, or personal visit.

Storing Data for Easy Access

Storing data that can be easily accessible is one of the most important things you can do when conducting any kind of investigation. After you have found information from your sources and library archives, categorizing it in a way that you can use it effectively is essential. At the end of each year, place all completed investigation files in clearly labeled storage boxes away from the main file area.

If you need more than one box, you can simply categorize the files alphabetically or by month. This frees your filing cabinet for the next year's investigations, while allowing you to have access to your archives. In many severe hauntings, paranormal activity may diminish or disappear altogether for months or years at a time, only to be rekindled for any number of reasons. If this happens, simply pull out the file on the haunting and put it in a new folder.

Before I bought a computer, I always put my important information on index cards and kept any newspaper clippings or photocopies in a file cabinet that was alphabetically separated by individual case. If I wanted some quick facts on a person or historical place, I simply went to the index card file box on my desk.

However, if I wanted more detailed information, I would consult the files in the cabinet. Of course, this was before computers became so easily available. Now, I just look up a file on the computer, and it saves so much space and time! I still keep photocopies of articles and letters from people in the file cabinet, but I also scan and categorize each and every one for a backup.

Although I now use computers to organize my files, I still use the same format to document information. The most important things to remember is to put the following information in your database.

Names

This section includes names of people directly involved in the paranormal events, those who lived in the house previously, or anybody that is suspected of being the spirit or ghost. Yes, it is possible to find out who a spirit or ghost actually was! Another good thing to put in this section is the contact information of the witnesses, just in case you need to get in touch with them at a future time.

Dates

This would include the dates you contacted the people involved in the paranormal events, when people moved in or out of a residence, or any other pertinent dates that you find. Also when a place was built would be included in this section. This is where becoming knowledgeable in history really is a benefit. You can even put in the era that a suspected apparition may have originated from (Civil War, Victorian, etc.). The more you know about the era, the better. You could identify a time period by the eyewitness' description of clothing, hairstyle, etc.

Locations

Of course, this means where the paranormal events take place. This section should include any history available on a location. Newspaper clippings that pertains to the location, blueprints (if available), and any other information about the surrounding area could be placed in this section of the file.

If you can, find out what the area looked like during the era that the apparition may have originated from. Buildings and places change over time.

For example, one of the ghosts that I investigated in 1996 was of a horseman who was seen galloping across the

Ohio River. This would appear to be rather odd behavior, even for an apparition! After doing some research on the area, it was found that a large covered bridge once stood in the area where the horseman was seen.

Types of Manifestations

It would be good to note any information about a paranormal event in this section. This way it would be easier to find any pattern, such as when the events take place, how often, etc. Note the frequency of the apparitions or other paranormal events, what actually takes place during an encounter, and any information you can gather from eyewitnesses, tape recordings, etc. You can organize the files in any way you wish, but this information is essential to document in one fashion or another.

Also, when you are finished investigating a haunting, hold on to your information! You just never know when you many need the notes again for a haunting in the future.

Three

PARANORMAL
PHOTOGRAPHY

Joseph Nicephore Niépce created the photographic process in June 1827. He began the research in to what became known as photography in 1817. It was common knowledge that silver salts had a chemical reaction to light, but most people considered it little more than a curiosity.

The first photograph was of a landscape that included the side of a building, a barn, and a tree. The image took over eight hours to develop. Soon after the photograph became noticed in certain scientific circles, Niépce went into a partnership with Louis Daguerre. Through continued research, they cut the time of developing a photograph from eight hours to less than one hour. Eventually, other people began to make strides in photographic techniques, making the camera available for people for the first time. The photographing of spirit forms came about by accident less than twenty years later.

The History of Paranormal Photography

The first documented report of paranormal photography came from Britain in 1862. William H. Mumler, a British photographer and engraver, had been experimenting with a camera, which at that time was simply a curiosity in affluent circles. Photography was just becoming a commonplace part of society. Mumler purchased a camera and began to use it by taking photographs of friends and family.

One day, as Mumler developed some photographs of family members, he noticed a very strange sight. Images of family members who had long been dead appeared on the same photograph as his living family members. He went to his family and confirmed that the images were of people that had died years ago, long before the camera had even been invented.

Up until this point, Mumler had no interest in or experience with the paranormal. He honed his techniques and soon began to make more and more photographs of deceased family members, friends, and acquaintances. Sometimes nothing appeared on the photographs he had taken; other times he had up to fifteen translucent portraits on a single picture. Most images were of family members and friends, but some were of complete strangers that neither

Mumler nor his family knew. The forms captured were usually out-of-focus portraits, although some photographs contained the common orbs, smoke, and apparitions that will be described in detail later. As the camera became more easily accessible for most people over the next few years, more and more people began to take their own photographs of incorporate entities. If one looks at the first photographs today with a critical eye, some can be easily explained away as feeble attempts at hoaxing, but a vast majority do appear to be authentic. Thus began the exciting and controversial phenomena of paranormal photography.

Photographs that contain paranormal manifestations are usually taken unknowingly by a diverse group of people. Most likely, there is no intention of capturing a ghost on film; they are taking photographs of loved ones, tour sites, or other things that interest them. However, photographing a spirit or ghost is also possible for the paranormal investigator. The specifics of the type of camera to use is found in the ghost-hunting kit section (see page 70).

Types of Photographic Manifestations

It would be prudent to discuss briefly the four different types of manifestations you can find on film. These manifestations are orbs, vortices, smoky forms or vapor, and apparitions. This section will offer a description and a sample of each type of photographic manifestation.

Orbs

Orbs are a common feature found in photographs of a haunted area. While the other appearances in photographs (such as smoky forms, apparitions, etc.) can actually depict an image of a ghost or spirit, orbs are a bit different. Orbs are not the actual images of a spirit or ghost, but instead an indication that an area contains a great deal of psychic energy.

In the typical photograph where they are found, orbs appear to be small- or medium-sized circles that are much lighter than the surrounding area. The number of orbs that are found in a photograph can range from one or two to over fifty, depending on the concentration of the psychic energy. Colors of the orbs generally have an off-white, yellow, blue, or red tint to them. Usually photographs of this type are taken at battlefields or cemeteries where a large number of people are buried, or places such as hotels, where people once congregated. Although the appearance of orbs does not necessarily indicate a haunting per se, they do occur more often in areas of paranormal or spiritual activity.

While at first glance the orbs appear to be similar to the circles created by refracted sunlight, upon closer inspection there are quite a number of factors that make psychic orbs a unique phenomenon. First, orbs appear to concentrate near or around the person or object that is emanating the psychic energy. Orbs near the epicenter may not necessarily be larger, but they are brighter, oftentimes nearly opaque. The further away from the source, the orbs become less and less distinct, and eventually fade into nothingness. Another difference between orbs and sunspots is that many of the photographs that contain orbs were taken in areas inconducive to the aforementioned sunspots. Some of the most impressive orb photographs were taken on overcast days, after dark, or inside, under subdued lighting conditions.

Orbs often appear near people who are fairly psychic, or places that have seen a great deal of intense emotional activity. When a photograph is taken of a medium, individuals who are involved in meditation or a spiritual ceremony, or of participants during a séance, there are often orbs in the photographs. Also, as in most hauntings, areas that have had intense emotional impressions (battlefields or other areas where people were injured, imprisoned, or died), these psychic orbs can be found easily. However, it is important to note that orbs are not the actual spirits or recordings. They often appear in conjunction with these apparitions, but developing photographs that have orbs is not proof positive that a place is haunted. It simply means that more investigation should be done and that you have a possible haunting. Orbs can appear on both digital and film cameras with similar frequency.

I have taken photographs of the orbs on many occasions. The most dramatic photograph was at a Civil War battle site outside of Charleston, West Virginia. After developing the pictures, I found over forty-two orbs that were clearly apparent on the film.

Although orbs are by far the most common types of paranormal phenomenon to be captured on film, if you are not aware and careful of the environment you are photographing, you may actually get some normal photographic features that could be easily confused for the real orbs. The following are three photographs. The first photograph is actually of a series of orbs that were taken in haunted area. Notice how round and clear they are. The second photograph is of falling snow. Many skeptics of paranormal photography will say that all orbs are the result of weather conditions, such as snow. Notice that the texture of the snow is entirely different than the texture of the orbs.

The final photograph is the refraction of sunlight that forms the sunspots. These look nothing like the orbs in ghost photography. Notice the overall shape of the sunspots. They are hexagonal as opposed to spherical. Also, they are lined in a row, instead of randomly appearing throughout the photograph. The final difference is the color of the hexagons. While the orbs are generally a milky or off-white color, the hexagons are reddish or orange in nature.

Vortices

Next to the orbs, the vortex is the most common type of paranormal event caught on film. They are generally found at the focal point of a haunted area; i.e., the location where

A photograph of orbs taken from an investigation. Notice the texture and pattern of the orbs that appear. Several orbs can appear in a single photograph. (© 1999 MAJDA)

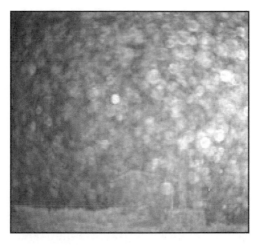

An example of snow in a photograph. There is no distinct pattern and the texture is much less concise than the orbs in the previous photograph. (© 1999, IGHS)

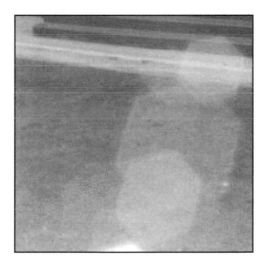

As the photograph indicates, sunspots usually appear in a straight line. In addition, sunspots also have a hexagonal shape, as opposed to the spherelike shape of the orbs. (© 1999, IGHS)

most of the ghostly activity occurs, and the center of the cold spot. Vortices are generally stationary, but have been photographed changing shape, getting larger and smaller, and occasionally forming extensions.

Amazingly, vortices sometimes cast a shadow, if the photographer is using a flash. The most common normal camera feature resembling the vortex is a camera strap in the photograph. (The photograph on page 49 shows a camera strap placed in front of the shutter.) Although the width and height of the strap is very similar to the vortex, the difference lies in the overall appearance. The strap is noticeably darker and more uniform in width. With the vortex, the shape generally tapers toward the bottom and the color is a bright white.

This is an example of the vortex apparition that appears in many paranormal photographs. It appears to be a very concentrated form of the vapor apparition. (© 1999, IGHS)

Smoky Forms or Vapor

The next type of paranormal manifestation commonly found on film is the smoky form. This is much more dramatic than orbs, but not as common. These manifestations are usually taken by accident. They are thought to be the actual spirit of a person, or even the aura of a living person. Almost as common as the vortex is what parapsychologists refer to as a "vapor."

This was the first type of phenomenon I photographed when I first became involved in ghost hunting. It is very similar to the vortex with a few exceptions. Instead of having a solid form, the vapor is actually more nebulous or smoke-like, although it does not have the consistency of cigarette or cigar smoke. It is almost as if it is in the process of

Camera straps are often mistaken for vortexes. Close observation will show many differences. For example, the strap does not taper toward the bottom of the photograph and is much darker than the vortex, which is generally a bright white color. (© 1999, IGHS)

forming a vortex. Sometimes a face or body part can be seen in the vaporous form, although most of the time it will appear very similar to the example in the following photograph. Cigarette smoke is somewhat less solid and wispier than the vapor form. Finally, when someone exhales in cold weather, the cloud can be easily photographed. It is much more condensed into a cloud form, instead of having a more distinct edge.

Generally, only one of two smoky forms will show up in a photograph and appear to concentrate on one person in the photograph. It is believed that the smoky forms are actually impressions of the recordings or auras of those who have passed on. Usually, smoky forms are involved in ghost hauntings, not spirit hauntings.

This is a classic example of the vapor or smoky form. Notice how there is a distinct outline on the outer edge of the form.
(© 1999 MAJDA)

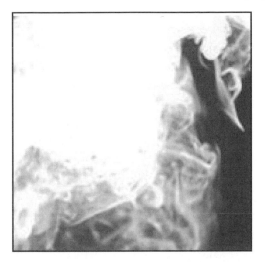

Although this photograph of cigarette smoke is similar to the vapor form, there are many differences. Notice how the smoke is much sharper and more defined around the edges than the vapor, which has a much softer appearance. (© 1999, IGHS)

Exhaled breath in cold weather can also be mistaken for a paranormal manifestation. In this case, the entire form is opaque and more solid than either the cigarette smoke or the vapor apparition. (© 1999, IGHS)

Apparitions

Another type of manifestation found in paranormal photographs is the apparition. This occurs when the actual form of the person or object appears on the film. Faces, clothing, and other identifying factors can readily be seen, although there was nothing paranormal detected when the area was photographed. When photographing an apparition, there will generally be a fully formed, clear individual, with one or more obvious body parts (legs, head, arms, etc.) missing.

One of the earliest and most famous photographs of an apparition shows the faces of James Courtney and Michael Meehan, two sailors from the S.S. *Watertown,* who were killed in December, 1924, when they were overcome by flames in a cargo tank. Courtney and Meehan were buried

S.S. *Watertown* Captain Keith Tracy took this photo from a series of six photographs, where the crew members claimed to have seen the apparitions of crew members Courtney and Meehan.

at sea. Shortly after, many of the crew members claimed to see their faces in the water by ship. Captain Keith Tracy took a series of six photographs where the crew members claimed to have seen the apparitions. This is the only photograph in which the apparitions of Courtney and Meehan appear. They were positively identified by friends and loved ones. The photographs have been authenticated on numerous occasions. To this day, the Tracy photograph remains one of the best pieces of evidence to support the theory that an apparition can be caught on film.

Another early photograph of a spirit was taken by Edward Wyllie in 1887. The subject was a gentleman by the name of J. R. Mercer. Apparently, the spirit apparitions were of his

The Wyllie photograph of 1887 was analyzed and discovered that it was touched up, especially around the areas of the "apparitions."

first wife and mother. In addition to the faces that appear, a handwritten message and a bouquet of flowers also appeared. This particular photograph was analyzed and evidence was found that it was touched up, especially around the areas of the "apparitions."

One of the most dramatic images I have seen of this type was given to me by a disc jockey who worked for a radio station that interviewed me on ghosts and spirits. It involves a man standing in a graveyard, overlooking a grave. The upper part of his body (baseball cap, flannel shirt, and arms) are easily noticeable. However, there is nothing from the thighs down. Upon closer examination of this photograph, it was found that the man in the photograph was actually someone who had recently died in an accident, and was standing before the grave of his father, who had died many years before.

Determining a Ghost Photograph's Authenticity

In the several years that I have been involved in ghost hunting, I have personally seen nearly a thousand ghost photographs that were taken by people who had a question about what may be appearing in a photograph. Others were novice investigators asking my opinion on a particular picture. A few were trying to test me to determine if I would call something paranormal when in fact they knew the photograph was normal.

Faking Photographs

As with any physical evidence associated with the paranormal, it is very important to determine its authenticity. If you are given a photograph from eyewitnesses or a third party, scrutinize the entire photography, including the area that captures the image. With the advances in computer technology, it is very easy to prepare a photograph so that it appears to have a ghost in it. Microsoft's Photoshop 4.0 is a very powerful program that has been used to make fake ghost photos that have fooled many professional ghost hunters in recent years.

If you are given a photograph of an alleged spirit or ghost, notice the type of paper that the picture is printed on. Check if the paper came from a photo-developing studio or a personal computer. Share the photograph with other people, asking their opinion. If you belong to a paranormal group, bring the photo to the meeting (making certain to retain the confidentiality of the people who took it) and ask the other members what their rendering is. Request the photograph's negative be examined if you doubt its authenticity.

Digital images are by far the easiest type of photographs to alter and falsify. Conventional cameras are more difficult to tamper with, although if somebody is knowledgeable in photography, a convincing photograph can be created. Polaroid "instamatics" are by far the most difficult to fake, and the paranormal images appear quite easily on this type of camera.

Hoaxes

During the late nineteen and early twentieth century, it was common for photographers to claim to photograph the spirits of loved ones close by. Since photography was still a new process to the commoners, it was indeed a very popular and lucrative business venture. Most photos were retouched after being developed. Usually, double exposures, props, or chances in the developing process were involved.

Today, photography has become much more advanced, and it is much harder to determine if a photograph has been tampered with. The two most common ways that a photograph can be faked are altering the length of exposure and adding images to the original photograph.

If the camera lens is manipulated to stay open for an extended period of time, the stationary parts of the photograph will remain clear while objects that have moved are transparent or blurry. Often, the transparent "spirit" can be made simply in this manner. Also, some ghost lights can be made in the same fashion with a flashlight or other bright source of light. When you examine a photograph, look at the entire picture for other objects that may move. If you are outside, look for the blur of vehicles or other objects that move. Often with a hoax of this nature, the hoaxers do not usually take into account background images.

Adding images or objects to the photograph is another way that photographers can capture a ghost or spirit on film. First, something can be added directly to a lens that can be put directly to the camera. A small cutout of a person standing, added to the lens itself, will create a shadow that can indeed be very realistic. Second, having someone dress in a manner similar to what the spirit has been reported to wear is also another way to fake a photograph. Third, an individual may purposely add images taken from other photographs, magazines, or any other visual media. This can be done while the film is being developed if the individual is processing the film himself. Also, a photograph of the photograph, with the images simply pasted on it, is another way it can be done. With the advent of digital imagery, individuals can use photo-editing software to create some very extensive and realistic faked photographs. When investigating, keep this in mind.

Advances in Paranormal Photography

It was common during the early twentieth century to photograph séances and other attempts at contacting the dead. Since those first paranormal photographs were taken, there have been many advances in photographic processes. The first cameras were very large and cumbersome, mounted on a tripod, and required the photographer to be under a large black cloth while focusing the area to be photographed. The first major advance was the manufacturing of cameras that were smaller and easier to transport. Once the camera became smaller and more mobile, people could then photograph areas that were very difficult to reach while carrying a large, bulky piece of equipment. (However, even with the portability issue solved, the photographs were only of mediocre quality, and still took a long time to develop.)

Perhaps the greatest step toward capturing a paranormal image on film was the introduction of the Polaroid camera in the 1960s. This camera was a marvelous piece of technology, allowing people to take pictures of virtually anything and to see the results in a matter of minutes. However, the Polaroid had one very interesting side effect. It was, and still is, absolutely one of the best types of cameras to use when attempting to capture an entity on film. It is not really known why ghosts and spirits can be so easily photographed using the Polaroid, but suffice it to say that it is a very important tool to use when investigating a haunting.

Recently, with the explosion of technology into mainstream society, there have been a number of other types of photographic equipment that have advanced the field of paranormal photography tremendously. One recent advancement in photography is the easy accessibility of infrared film for 35mm cameras. This type of film has captured as many paranormal presences as the Polaroid camera. The infrared film is used to capture the heat signatures and alterations in temperature of an area rather than an actual visual image. Since most haunted areas have a distinct difference in temperature, the infrared camera can actually capture the extent that there is a marked difference in an area. Another great advance in photography is the introduction of the digital camera. The camera is used to take photographs that can be directly uploaded onto a personal computer. There is no need to purchase film at all.

Four

ELECTRONIC VOICE PHENOMENON

Electronic Voice Phenomenon (EVP) is an aspect of ghost hunting that should definitely not be overlooked. It involves the actual recording of disembodied sounds and voices picked up in a haunted area. If done correctly, the results can be truly fascinating and can give you critical information regarding the haunting.

The Beginnings of Electronic Voice Phenomenon

The practice of purposefully listening for disembodied voices to communicate with deceased loved ones has its origins in the séances of the late nineteenth and early twentieth century. During the séances that were popular during the Victorian era, the medium would use funnels, horns, and other devices to attempt to produce a voice from the spirit world. In the typical séance, the medium would ask the spirit to make his or her presence known through a sound such as a trumpet or horn, then proceeding to a drum, and finally making its voice heard to everyone in the room. The voices would start as a whisper, and gradually become louder at the medium's command. The voices would often assure concerned loved ones that the spirits were happy and well. The spirits contacted also wished to convey to the séance participants that they were protectedand keeping a close eye on them. This consolation was generally enough to pacify all but the most skeptical of séance participants.

Debunkers investigating the séances often found that the medium had an assistant well hidden someplace within the room. The trumpets and funnels were often attached to strings that caused them to float in full sight of the séance participants. When the medium summoned the spirit to make a sound through the trumpet, the assistant would often comply. Finally, the messages from the "departed" were generally very vague in order to cover as many people as possible.

Those interested in the occult and spirit communication often tried to find a way to speak with the spirit world without the necessity of a séance. In the 1920s, Thomas Edison earnestly attempted to construct a spirit communicator, in order to speak with what has been termed the "living impaired." Although a few prototypes were created, all attempts met with failure. Shortly thereafter, Edison passed away. According to the medium Sigram Seuterman, Edison made contact in 1967, in hopes to continue work on the spirit communicator he began when alive. Little more was heard from Seuterman after several requests were made by people throughout the world for the construction of Edison's spirit communicator.

In addition, shortly before his death, Nikola Tesla also became interested in communication with spirits. This inventor actually built a communications device and claimed to have had some success speaking with the spirit world. However, before he was able to discuss his findings with many people, the great inventor died.

Like the first paranormal photographs, the first recordings of discarnate voices took place quite unintentionally. The first documented case of an EVP takes place in 1959, with a man attempting to record bird songs along the countryside in Sweden. Fredrich Jurgenson had very little interest in recording spirit voices; he simply wanted to make a recording of bird sounds in their natural habitat. When Jurgenson played back the bird songs, he was amazed to have recorded the sound of a man speaking Norwegian about the songs of nocturnal birds. Jurgenson attempted other recordings and, although he heard nothing at the time of the recording, upon playing back the tape, he had picked up other voices. He claimed that the voices sounded different than regular human voices. The speed of the voices were always much faster than voices used in normal conversation.

Due to the technology of the time, a person without rooms of equipment could not simply record a voice at a higher speed and superimpose it onto another recording.

This completely fascinated him, and within a fairly short period of time had collected a large number of recordings of disembodied voices.

Five years later, in 1964, Jurgenson published *Voices from the Universe*. This drew quite a bit of attention to Jurgenson, and immediately piqued the interest of Konstantin Raudive, a Latvian psychologist who was interested in paranormal phenomena. The two met in 1965 and Raudive started to make his own voice recordings. Over the next twenty years, Raudive claimed to have recorded over 100,000 voices of people from all walks of life and nationalities. His findings were published in the 1971 book *Breakthrough*. Due to his contributions to the recording of disembodied voices, Electronic Voice Phenomenon is sometimes still referred to as "Raudive voices."

As the quality of recording devices improved and more types of recorders became available, the variety of the EVP recordings also increased. Not only were people able to hear voices ranging from a few whispers that were barely audible to very loud and clear voices, some also began to record a metallic-sounding voice. Many experts analyzed these samples of the new generation of EVP with mixed results.

Some believed that the voices were created using synthesizers and computers to alter a living person's voice. Granted, many of the metallic voices do sound as if they were manufactured with a computer instead of being recorded directly from a haunted area. Other experts believed that the metallic voices were spirits using the recording device itself as a voice amplifier. People who have lost loved ones, and have heard the metallic voices, claim that with the exception of the metallic tone, the voice is almost identical to the deceased loved one.

My First Experience with EVP

When I first began to investigate hauntings, I was very open-minded about many things that people claimed to have experienced, but I was very doubtful about the existence of the actual recording of disembodied voices. I believed that the majority of recordings I had heard in the past were either unintentional recordings of overheard conversations or outright fabrications. I'm not certain *why* I could not fathom EVP when I could easily understand and accept spirit photography, séances, and hauntings in general. I suppose that I could believe only so much, and had to draw the line somewhere.

However, on a hot, summer day in July 1990, I was asked to participate in an investigation with a friend who had heard of a very strong haunted area. After many long discussions, I reluctantly agreed to bring a tape recorder to the investigation site. We were investigating an old, abandoned farmhouse in the country about ten miles outside of Ripley. There had been some sightings by at least five people of a little girl in a long nightgown wandering around the farmhouse over the last several weeks. We had checked the history of the farmhouse and had found that there had been a little girl named Rebecca who had died of a long illness in the house in the late 1880s.

After taking photographs with a Polaroid Instamatic and having nothing show up on the film, I finally agreed to place the tape recorder in the area we considered the "cold spot." As mentioned elsewhere, the cold spot is generally in an area that has the most ghostly activity. There was a fresh ninety-minute Maxell audiocassette placed in the Sony shoebox tape recorder. After making certain that the batteries were new, we left the house to grab a bite of lunch.

When we felt enough time had passed, we returned to the house to pick up our tape recorder and head home. The summer sun was beating down on us, and we were tired. We packed up our equipment and started to drive home. My friend placed the cassette into a Walkman and started to listen while I drove.

About twenty minutes later, he screamed and told me to pull to the side of the road. After I did so, he handed the cassette player over for me to take a listen. What I heard was nothing short of amazing. There was a faint sound of a cough and a little girl asking for her "mama." I looked at my friend in disbelief. I was certain that the cassette had not been tampered with and was positive that it was the same cassette because it had my handwriting on it. We had actually picked up the voice of a little girl who had died over a hundred years before. Since that day, I have *always* used a cassette recorder in my investigations.

Effectively Investigating with EVP

The first thing to do when examining an EVP is to determine if the source of the voice is coming from a ghost recording or from a spirit. In a ghost haunting, the voices are usually impressions left by the individual. With very few exceptions, there is no real attempt to communicate with the living. It is as if an investigator is eavesdropping over a conversation that has taken place at some point in the past. The voice is not directed toward anybody in particular, as in the case of a ghost recording.

As for spirits, the phenomenon may be slightly different. The spirit may be actually attempting to communicate with the living. The information appears to be directed toward someone in the room. It could be as simple as a message to a loved one, or as complex as a series of instructions to be followed.

Although producing an EVP during an investigation may sound fairly complicated, it is really a very simple procedure. All you need are some high-quality blank cassette tapes, a tape recorder (preferably with a multispeed, playback function), a microphone, fresh batteries or a reliable power source, and a great deal of patience. When doing an investigation, a great deal of the work actually takes place before setting up the tape recorder. You will need to find out some information about the haunting to find the best conditions for your EVP investigation.

First, determine which room you would like to use to record the EVP. Usually, this is the room with the highest frequency of paranormal activity. If you are not certain which area is the most active, try to find the area that feels the coldest.

A very important thing to research prior to recording the EVP is to find the time of day that the paranormal activity takes place most often. This can be found out through interviewing any eyewitnesses. If you are not certain of the time of higher paranormal activity, try to find a time where there is the lowest chance of any outside disturbance. This would include visitors to the area, people coming in and out, pets, etc. In the case of EVP, the less traffic through the area, the better.

Some investigators prefer a source of white noise in the background to make the voices stand out. White noise is simply a steady background sound such as a dripping faucet, radio static, or an electric fan. Although I have recorded EVP like this, I personally prefer *not* to use white noise in the background. I have found there to be no difference in the quality of recordings in either case. However, experiment using both techniques and stick with the one that you are most comfortable with.

Once you are certain that the area you are recording will be free of passersby or traffic, place the cassette player in a place where it can be very easily seen. If you would like, you can place a bit of flour around it to make certain that nobody will tamper with it. Also, if you are certain that there will be no chance that there will be any tampering of the tape recorder, you can investigate other parts of the house while the recorder is running. It is generally a good idea not to have a cassette longer than ninety minutes. The 120-minute cassettes have a tendency to stretch and break. I've found that sixty-minute chrome cassettes work the best, and pick up the most EVP.

After the cassette has played entirely through, return to the cassette player. Clean up any flour that you may have placed in the area and rewind the cassette. Once the cassette is rewound, you may want to pull out a set of headphones and plug into the headset to minimize any distractions from outside sources. Turn the volume up to the highest setting and listen closely to anything you may have recorded. A good idea is to close your eyes while listening because you will be more focused.

If you pick up anything, rewind a second time so that you can listen to it again. If you have a tape counter, note the number so you can find the EVP easily again. The EVP will generally be very faint and you may have to strain to hear it. Generally, the EVP tends to sound like a whisper. Occasionally, the voice will be recorded at a different speed and may sound either slower or faster than normal. Listen to the voice a number of times until you can determine what is being said. Generally, it will be a small part of a conversation that has taken place many years before, but occasionally a message will be directed toward someone living. Allow other people in the group to listen and ask their opinion. Once you've arrived at a decision about the EVP, do not forget to write the information in your notebook. Be certain to include the date, time, cassette tape counter number, people present, and as much information about the voice as possible.

Be patient and thorough when listening to the cassette tape. You may feel like fast forwarding for a few seconds, but it is important to listen to every minute of the cassette. One thing that new ghost hunters tend to overlook when they encounter their first few EVP is to listen to the entire tape. The second time I had ever recorded an EVP, I neglected to listen to the rest of the tape, and nearly missed two other recordings.

Five

YOUR GHOST-
HUNTING KIT

It is generally a good idea to have a
variety of tools (and people) at your dis-
posal. I have found that my own investigative methods tend to lean toward the scientific. Although I have on occasion picked
up on psychic impressions, I like having
detailed data. A photograph of a ghost
cannot be denied, once all other possible
causes for the image have been eliminated,
of course! A psychic can keep detailed
notes as well, but it does help the case to
have more than one source to document
the experience. As a scientific ghost hunter,
I have found certain tools very useful.

It is not essential to have the most expensive, high-tech equipment that professional parapsychologists may use; it is possible to do very well with a kit of basic and inexpensive equipment.

Here are some of the items that have been most useful to me over the years.

Cameras

One of the best items to have in your inventory is a camera. There are three basic types of cameras to consider when building your ghost hunting kit. Each camera has benefits and drawbacks, and each should be taken into consideration before making a final buying decision. The three types are the Polaroid instant cameras, 35mm cameras, and digital cameras.

Instant Cameras

Instant cameras, particularly the Polaroid SX-70 One-Step, are the best types of cameras for ghost photography. The instant cameras have two major benefits. First, the photograph is developed within a minute of taking it. Second, a ghost image on a film negative may be considered a flaw by professional film developers, and they may attempt to correct it, or simply won't develop the print. Photo-developing companies may discard photographs and negatives that have streaks or cloudy images. Since this is what usually appears in a spirit or ghost photograph, this can pose a problem when they possibly destroy your evidence.

The best position for the camera is to point it directly toward an abnormally cold spot, or where the apparition is witnessed most often. This usually is where the spirit or ghost is felt or sensed the most.

Total Cost for Polaroid Instamatic Cameras

A Polaroid Instamatic camera will usually cost between $40 and $50, depending on the specific model and where you purchase the camera. Another thing to take into account is the film for the Polaroid camera. The film is much more expensive then 35mm camera film. Generally, you can find a pack of ten exposures for $10–$15.

35mm Cameras

These cameras are very easy to find and very easy to use. Any department store will have a large variety of 35mm cameras. Depending on your budget and taste, you can opt for a basic unit, or purchase a more advanced unit. For the beginner, a smaller camera would be sufficient, but if you wanted to have the option of a zoom lens, red-eye reduction, or other features, consider getting a more expensive camera.

If you do use a 35mm camera, use a film with a higher speed. I recommend a speed of 1600 or 3200. Also, if possible, set your camera's aperture for higher openings, as you would normally do for night photography. The lens will let in more light and increase the chance of capturing a ghost or spirit on film. As for the shutter speed, I would use the fastest speed possible. In most 35mm cameras, you can go up to 1/500 second.

There are some solutions for this. If you know about photography, you can take photographs with black and white film and develop the negatives yourself. Or you can tell your film processor that you want the negatives and photographs untouched despite any "flaws" that may be present.

> **High Film Speed:** 1600 or 3200 speed
> **Lens Opening:** Highest possible opening
> **Shutter Speed:** Fastest possible for your camera

Total Cost for 35mm Cameras

You can pay between $15 and $30 for a no-frills camera. For the higher quality pieces, you will naturally pay more. The more you invest does not necessarily mean better photographs. I've seen photographs that were taken with $20 cameras that were just as professional, if not more so, than their $200 counterparts.

The film for the 35mm camera is fairly inexpensive, often being between $3 and $5 per roll of twenty-four exposures. Remember that to get the most effective paranormal photographs, use a higher speed film.

Digital Cameras

Digital cameras are quickly becoming the camera of choice among paranormal investigators. You don't have to worry about film, can view the image as soon as it is taken, and can download the image directly to your computer.

You can purchase some rudimentary digital cameras for as low as $70, but there is no image preview and the resolution is not very clear. Some people are very adept at graphic design, and can alter a digital image to give the appearance of an apparition.

When shopping for a digital camera, pay close attention to see if the camera is compatible with your computer system.

Total Cost for Digital Cameras

Depending on how elaborate you want your digital system to be, the cost will range from $70 to over $1,000. I would not recommend purchasing the least expensive cameras because of the resolution and overall quality leaves much to be desired.

Anything from $200 and higher would more than likely be useful for your investigations. Notice the resolution of the camera; a good rule of thumb is the higher the resolution, the better quality picture you will take.

Tape Recorder

A tape recorder is another very important piece of equipment. It should have a microphone sensitive enough to pick up faint sounds at a distance. You can find an external microphone for a reasonable price in many department and electronics stores. It is beneficial, but not necessary, to use a machine that is voice-activated and has a tape counter. A microcassette recorder (the kind used for taking personal notes) is ideal for ghost hunting. It is compact, yet can pick up very slight sounds. Make certain that you have at least two extra blank tapes and a fresh set of batteries at all times in your kit.

There are many different uses for the tape recorder. When placed in a strategic spot, the machine may record incorporeal voices and sounds. The most effective way to use a tape recorder for this purpose is not to carry it around, but to place it near where most of the manifestations originate. (Please note: Electronic equipment tends to malfunction when it passes through a cold spot.)

The tape recorder can also be used to record eyewitness accounts for future reference. Sometimes when you are note-taking, you can ignore small, seemingly insignificant details, but these could prove to be very important later. Also, the recording will allow you to examine a person's story and compare it with those of other eyewitnesses. Some very convincing hoaxes have been uncovered simply by taking a very close look at eyewitnesses' conflicting testimonies.

Total Cost for Tape Recorders
Between $15 and $45, plus batteries and blank cassettes.

Microwave Radiation or Electromagnetic Detectors

These tools are not as expensive as they sound. Any large department store should have a microwave radiation detection unit in the appliance section. The normal use for the unit is to detect radiation leaks in microwave ovens. The most common type of microwave radiation detector on the market today is the "Detecto Card" from the Enzone Corporation. It is a credit-card-sized instrument with a radiation-sensitive strip along one side. To use it, simply follow the directions on the back of the card.

Since the unit detects a change in the amount of radiation in an area, it should show a noticeable difference when it encounters an abnormal energy field (cold spots, electric light and appliance malfunctions, and so on). Sometimes, an energy field is not associated with a spirit, but more often than not you'll find increased spiritual activity around places with high concentrations of energy, such as ley lines or power lines.

Electromagnetic detectors are very similar to radiation detectors, but they focus on electromagnetic energy as opposed to microwave radiation. Electromagnetic fields emanate from virtually everything electrical: televisions, computers, VCRs, people (auras), and even spirits and ghosts.

Again, the Enzone Corporation has a useful unit for approximately $30. It will detect even a slight disturbance in the area's electromagnetic fields. One note of caution—the original intent of the device is to detect electromagnetic fields from such items as appliances, computers, etc. When doing a reading for spirits, try not to confuse the readings of one of these normal objects with signs of spiritual or ghostly activity.

Total Cost for Detecto Cards
Between $4 and $6.

Total Cost for Electromagnetic Field Detectors
About $30.

Pad of Paper and Pen

Pen and paper are invaluable tools for anyone doing any type of research, paranormal or otherwise. These can be used to sketch a map of the area you are investigating, take notes, or record observations and data. Also, it is wise to write down any random thoughts that you have while investigating a haunted area. They could be a spirit's way of attempting to communicate with you.

Total Cost for Pen and Paper
Between $1 and $4.

Compass

A compass has many uses in ghost hunting. First, it will provide you with an orientation of the surroundings. This is especially helpful when orienting a map of the area, because it keeps things in perspective and lessens the chance of getting lost.

Second, it can also be used as a "spirit detector" in a pinch. Just as spirits may cause electrical problems with their surroundings, they also can create havoc with magnetic sources, such as your compass. The needle may start to go haywire or refuse to work. It may also point toward the spirit, although this is not very common.

Total Cost for Compass
Between $5 and $10.

Watch or Stopwatch

The use for a watch is obvious. It can be used to record the time into your notebook or journal, the length of a particular phenomenon or tape recording, or just to check the time. You don't need any special type of watch, any wristwatch will do.

One function that most digital watches have today would be the stopwatch feature. The stopwatch can give you a much more accurate time than simply using the second hand on the analog models.

Total Cost for Watch
$5 and above.

Laptop Computer

In this world of advanced technology, having access to a computer at any given time is both easier and less expensive than one may think. One of the tools particularly beneficial while conducting research is a laptop computer. Laptops come in a number of sizes, ability, and prices. A quick online search can find a decent system for $600 or less. My own Compaq Presario 1235 cost only $400 and is more than adequate for my purposes in ghost hunting and writing. With the constant upgrade in computers, systems that were top of the line only one or two years ago are all but obsolete, which would make finding a good laptop fairly easy. However, that being the case, there are some bare minimums that you should have in order to have enough computer for your needs. A system should have *at least* the following specifications:

Windows 95 or higher
133 MHz or better
64 MB of RAM, or better
1.44 floppy drive
12 x CD-ROM, or better
2-gigabyte hard drive, or better
56K modem

It is true that you can find a system with less RAM, no CD-ROM, and a smaller hard drive, but for the small amount of extra money you would spend for these features, it would be well worth it to go ahead and find a system that could suit your purposes better.

Today, virtually all programs are on CD-ROM, and some of the older word-processing and database systems are obsolete and cannot be read by newer systems. This could be a problem when you are trying to transfer information from the laptop to a desktop computer.

One thing to take into account when searching for a laptop is that the most expensive units are not necessarily the best, especially if you are working in the field and spending a great deal of time with your computer system. The major purpose of the laptop is to store information and to keep in touch with other members of your group via e-mail. Check into used or refurbished equipment. Many laptops are available on the Internet and at computer stores that would more than adequately serve your purpose. Although nobody wants to have his or her computer stolen or destroyed, it is definitely something to take into account when looking into a laptop. Again, a used or refurbished system would be easier to replace than a top-of-the-line system.

The 2-gig hard drive is necessary for a number of reasons. First, many of the programs that you will be using (Microsoft Word, Excel, etc.) can take up a fairly large amount of space on a hard drive. Additionally, if you are going to be investigating with a digital camera, it would be better to have the space to upload any images you have taken. When doing an investigation in which I use a digital camera, I upload the images on a daily basis so I can examine each image and can clear up the memory on the camera for the next day's investigation.

A 56K modem would also be a highly recommended feature on any laptop that you look for. In many cases, your investigation may take you from your home base for an extended period of time. With the modem, you can connect to any phone jack and send images, files, and e-mails to other members in your group. When using the modem, make certain that the phone line you use is analog. If the line is digital, there is a good chance your computer could be damaged.

When I first became involved in ghost hunting, I went to the library and other places for information, and found myself copying everything freehand onto a legal pad. Once I got home, I typed all of the notes I had written into my PC, which took nearly as long as taking the notes in the first place. With the laptop, I can simply type and organize any information directly to my word-processor program.

I have a particular procedure when writing or conducting any research in the field. Once I finish typing my information into the laptop, I always make a copy of the file onto a floppy disk right on the spot. Then, I place the disk in a location other than the laptop carrying case. In the event that the laptop is damaged, lost, or stolen, I would still have the information that may have taken hours to put together. It is better to be safe than sorry.

Another thing to take into account is the compatibility of your laptop to your desktop or to the desktops belonging to other people in your group. I tend to synchronize my two systems, updating each of them at the same time to prevent any incompatibility problems. If you have to convert a document from one type of program to another (WordPerfect to Microsoft Word, for example), you may very well get "dingbats" through the conversion. "Dingbats" are the symbols that sometimes appear during a conversion process. You can also lose some information such as justification, page breaks, alignments, fonts, etc., during a conversion. Granted, while most of these are fairly easy to rectify, they can be time consuming and should be avoided whenever possible.

Flour

Although flour may appear to be a rather unorthodox tool at first, it can nonetheless be an important part of your ghost-hunting kit. Depending on the nature of the investigation, you may have to prevent tampering with the area you are investigating, and flour would be an inexpensive item to use. After you have placed your equipment in the location that you want, sprinkle flour at the base of the item to four feet out from the item. If somebody tampers with the equipment, he or she will very likely disturb the flour.

The flour can also be used to determine if a paranormal event is taking place. If you are fairly certain that the area is secure from being tampered with, you can sprinkle flour in the area that has the highest frequency of paranormal events. Keep a close eye on this area, as the spirit may leave impressions in the flour. Use the flour in this area only if you are *certain* that there will be no physical tampering involved.

If you decide to use flour, make certain that you clean up the area completely when you are finished. To not clean up an area reflects badly on the paranormal investigator and denotes a sense of unprofessionalism that may follow you to future cases.

Thread

This is also an inexpensive item that can be used to determine that your equipment is not tampered with. Again, before leaving your equipment (especially recording devices and cameras), tape thread around the area surrounding the piece of equipment. If possible, place your equipment in a corner so that you can use the walls to tape the thread to. Also mark where you placed the tape or put a small piece of paper so that it is barely hanging from the tape. If the thread is moved by somebody that is tampering with your equipment, they may not notice the small mark that you placed for the tape and in their hurry will not place it in the exact same spot.

Along the same lines, the small piece of paper (no larger than a thumbnail) will probably fall to the floor undetected if the thread is moved. If the thread is moved, the tape is placed in a different place, or if the piece of paper has dropped to the floor, assume that your equipment has been tampered with. In any case, do not let the person allowing you to investigate the area know that you taped the thread around the area.

If your equipment has been tampered with . . .

In either case, if you find that your equipment has been tampered with, the first thing to do is to inform your group of your suspicions. Meet with your group members in private, well away from any residents who may be in the area. The key here is discretion. If you decide that your equipment has been tampered with purposefully, calmly pack up the equipment and inform that people that called you that the investigation has concluded. Explain to them that the equipment has been tampered with and calmly leave. Please keep in mind that all people present may not be involved in the tampering, and be aware that the reactions will range from feigned surprise to disgust to outright admission. In any case, be professional and leave as promptly as possible. Once you decide to leave, keep all the contact information and files in case you are approached by these people again, and refuse to conduct another investigation for them.

You may find that there are many more pieces of equipment that you personally would like to see in your ghost-hunting kit, but the items described here are just a starter kit. The total cost for the kit listed above ranges from $50 to $100, depending on specific types of equipment you choose to purchase. However, the research, hands-on experience, photographs, and data that can be produced with this equipment are invaluable!

By no means are you limited to these few items. Other things that you may take along on your ghost-hunting expeditions might include any of the following: flashlight, first-aid kit, cell phone, etc. Again, good luck on your first few expeditions searching for ghosts and spirits!

Six

FORMING A
PARANORMAL GROUP

Ghost hunting has become a popular activity in many locations throughout the United States and Europe. In response, it is not uncommon to find ghost-hunting organizations being formed, especially in and around towns of historical significance.

Finding an Existing Group

To find a ghost-hunting or paranormal group, you may only have to call your local library. You can also do an online search for groups in your area. Some sites that may help are listed in Appendix B. Local Unitarian Universalist churches may be another good source of information. Even if the church does not hold meetings of this type, church officials may point you to one. Many community bookstores, colleges, and universities also host ghost groups, or even classes on parapsychology.

No two organizations are alike when it comes to investigating a haunting. One ghost-hunting or paranormal group may stay very close to the scientific method, only taking into consideration tangible, measurable evidence. Another group may be more metaphysical in nature, relying on intuition, psychic gifts, and forms of divination to learn about a house or haunting.

I have found it beneficial to be involved in a group that is a combination of the scientific and metaphysical. An investigative group that is entirely scientific in nature may miss many subtle but important clues, such as impressions and feelings. A sense of sorrow or dread, or other psychic impressions left in a particular room, cannot be measured on scientific instruments, but can be picked up by ESP. However, if the group solely relies on the metaphysical, it risks the possibility of transforming intuition into imagination. Natural phenomena such as creaks and drafts can be interpreted as information picked up "psychically" from a spirit or ghost. With a combination of the two types of investigation styles—scientific and metaphysical—readings and intuition tend to validate each other, and can make a difference in determining whether a real haunting is taking place.

Forming a Paranormal Group

Potential members for a paranormal group can be found in all professions and walks of life. The supernatural has become a very popular topic of conversation. Each year, more and more people are developing a strong interest in learning about this phenomenon, and experiencing supernatural events on their own.

To find quality members for your paranormal group, the first thing to do is to determine exactly what your group meetings will encompass. Will you take a classic case from the pages of parapsychology (Borley Rectory, for example) to examine it? Will your group be more of a discussion group in which all people have the opportunity to offer their opinions, views, and personal accounts? Will you form an experiential group in which you conduct experiments and share tips or techniques on how to do an effective ghost hunt? You can even make your own group free-form, with a variety of different topics and styles for the meetings to follow. As you can see, the limits of the type of paranormal group to form are virtually limitless.

Once you determine how you want your group to be formed, the next step is to determine a meeting time and place. Meeting times are usually best in the early evenings or weekend afternoons and should last between sixty to ninety minutes. If the meeting lasts longer, the members may get bored or tired. Shorter, more frequent meetings can be more productive.

Next, let the general public know about your group. Put out flyers where people congregate and where you can get attention. Laundromats, colleges, bars and pubs, libraries, and bookstores are very good places. Also, you can contact local newspapers and radio stations to see if they can make an announcement for your group.

Use your imagination. One friend of mine formed a group and printed business card-size announcements. She then placed them in occult and paranormal books at the local mall's bookstore. The plan was very discreet but very effective. It was pleasantly surprising how many people joined the group by this method.

After you have begun your membership drive, it would be good to determine how each member can assist the group. Some people are great at graphic design and can develop brochures, flyers, etc. Others may be proficient at public speaking and would be wonderful at making public appearances with the media and other groups.

Ask each member what he or she likes to do or is good at; try to find an activity that they can perform that is somehow related to their interests. Be careful not to mismatch people with something they do not like or are not good at. If you are not careful and this happens, your group may be in jeopardy of falling apart in a very short time due to member dissatisfaction.

Try not to make the group too large; usually five to fifteen people is the perfect size for a paranormal investigation group. However, if you do find that more people are interested in your group, you can simply have group meetings and have discussions about various paranormal phenomena. There is a difference between a paranormal discussion group and a paranormal investigation group. I helped to create one group that had close to thirty members. Since it was a large area, we decided that everybody would be assigned to five smaller groups, based on their interest and expertise. One group worked better with haunted houses, another expressed an interest and aptitude with cemeteries, a third would concentrate on poltergeist activity, etc. It worked well for the length of time the group was together.

There should be a sense of order and professionalism in your group no matter the size. Meetings should begin promptly at the appointed time. An agenda should be followed, even if it means simply having a free-form philosophical discussion. If there are any necessary projects or tasks that need completing, they should be discussed and distributed to participating members. Without a basic format for the meetings, your group will eventually stop functioning properly, people will lose interest, and the group will fold.

Membership requirements are entirely dependent on each specific group. Some groups allow anybody to join, while others have age limitations due to liability factors. (I prefer the open memberships, where anybody who wants to join is allowed to, providing they have an open mind and are not there to cause problems.) However, keep in mind that excluding anybody simply because of gender, sexual orientation, race, religious affiliation is not the proper way to conduct a group (and also may be illegal).

Once you have enough members in your group, it might be valuable to elect officers. There are four necessary positions that should be filled: president, vice president, treasurer, and secretary. The president calls the meeting to order and is the head chairperson of all meetings. The vice president will assist the president in his or her duties, and conduct meetings in the president's absence. The secretary will take minutes of the meeting and prepare any necessary paperwork for the meetings (handouts, photocopies, etc.). The treasurer is responsible for any finances that may come into the group (membership dues, contributions, etc.). Other committees or positions may be formed as the need

arises and could include such things as a publicity committee, membership drive coordinator, or paranormal activity
authentication committee.

A wonderful book that would help immensely with forming your group is *Robert's Rules of Order*. This book goes
step-by-step through conducting meetings in the parliamen-
tary procedure fashion. Granted, some of the material in the
book will not apply to your group, but some will give you
ideas about fine-tuning the workings of your group.

Keep in mind that forming an effective paranormal group
can be a very detailed and time-consuming task. If you have
little experience in running or forming a group, it might be
an idea to attend group meetings from other organizations
to observe how meetings are conducted. As in the case of
ghost hunting, always stay open-minded, be observant, and
be willing to communicate with people when conducting
meetings. The extra effort that you put forth will be noticed
and appreciated.

Appendix A
Forms and Questionnaires

To make your first investigations run more smoothly, it would be a good idea to keep all of your information organized so you are able to access it at a moment's notice. Over the years, I have developed a series of forms that have helped me immensely when I was trying to keep my notes together. Each form is used specifically for a different part of the investigation.

Form One is simply a permission form signed by both the ghost hunter and the owner/resident of the area being investigated. It is designed to protect both the investigator and the owner/resident in the case of an accident. By signing this, the owner/resident allows the paranormal group members listed on the form permission to study and research the area. The investigators should explain the procedure used in examining a haunted area so that there are no surprises on behalf of the owner/resident. Answer any questions that he or she may have. Form One is also to protect the owner/resident because it holds liable any member of the ghost hunter team for any property that is broken or defaced as a result of the investigation.

Form Two is used specifically to interview the eyewitnesses of a haunting. The questions on the form are written in order for the investigator to make certain that nothing is overlooked during the interview. It provides space for the location's history, the people who are experiencing paranormal events, a description for the specific events, and much other essential information. The first part of Form Two should be discussed with the eyewitnesses and any questions should be answered. The second section of Form Two is not to be shared with the eyewitnesses. It allows space for the investigator to write down any observations or impressions that he or she may have on the people being interviewed. This is particularly valuable if another investigator needs to take over an investigation for any reason.

Form Three is the research questions that need to be answered when doing research in the library or other areas. These are important questions about the origins of the house, the previous tenants, and any history that may be important to the investigation. It also has a section to write down anything peculiar that you may find in your research.

Form Four is the ghost-hunter's checklist. It is simply a reminder of what to bring when investigating a haunted area. The list includes a space for any ghost-hunting equipment, a list of people in the investigative team, and the condition of the location being haunted. It also has a specific section for documenting any paranormal events that the investigators may encounter.

Form Five is a very important form. It is the description of paranormal events, used by the investigators when they conduct a tour and investigation of an area allegedly haunted. Use this form to write down notes about the condition of the house, the impressions you may get from a particular area, etc.

Lastly, *Form Six* is the results of investigation form. This is used to make a conclusion about the eyewitnesses, physical conditions of the house, a description of any paranormal events that may have taken place, and your group's professional opinion of what has been encountered.

These forms have been designed over a period of years through trial and error. I have found them most valuable in my investigations. The forms can be photocopied or altered in any way to assist ghost hunters in their investigating; they are simply a template to give you ideas. If you do decide to make changes to the forms, please keep in mind that the information should still be included in some way.

Form One: Permission to Investigate

I, _____, hereby give permission to allow access to the location at the following addresses:

_____

_____

_____

for the purpose of conducting an investigation into possible paranormal occurences and conducting field research at this location. The investigator and any individuals accompanying the investigator hereby release the owner from any and all liability for injuries and/or damages that occur during the investigation. The investigator _____ also assumes responsibility for any and all damages to the property during the investigation.

Owner_____ Date _____

Printed name _____

Investigator_____ Date _____

Printed name _____

Form Two: Questionnaire for
Paranormal Encounters – Interview Questions

Date of Inteview:_____ Name of Investigator:_____

Location Information

Physical Address of Investigation: _____

History of Location (date built, previous occupants, battles or other con-
frontations near location, other paranormal phenomena, etc.):

_____

_____

_____

_____

_____

Documentation of any previous paranormal accounts (newspaper clippings, occupants' testimony, etc.):

_____

_____

_____

_____

_____

Attach drawing or map of location to sheet, and mark areas that show
paranormal activity.

Occupant Information

Number of Occupants at Location:_____

Names, gender, and birthdates of occupants (add additional to back of
sheet):

1. _____
2. _____
3. _____
4. _____
5. _____

Contact information of occupants:

Phone: _____ E-mail address: _____

Mailing address:

_____

_____

_____

How long have occupants lived at location? _____

Have any of the occupants encountered any of the following? (Check all that apply.)

❑ Voices (if yes, explain:_____)

❑ Smells/Odors (if yes, explain: _____)

❑ Shadows (if yes, explain: _____)

❑ Orbs

❑ Smoky Forms

❑ Strong Random Thoughts

❑ Cold or Hot Spots (if yes, explain: _____)

❑ Recent Death of Loved One (if yes, give info:_____)

❑ Recent Anniversary of Loved One's Death, Birthday, Anniversary, etc.

❑ Rappings or Knockings

❑ Mood Changes, especially in one room (if yes, explain: _____)

❑ Conversations with Spirit (if yes, explain: _____)

❑ Door(s) Opening/Closing

❑ Moving/Disappearing Objects

❑ Electrical Disturbances (frequent light bulb burnouts, etc.)

❑ Puberty of Family Member or Emotional Stress of Adolescents in Area

❑ Renovations in Location (if yes, explain: _____)

❑ Problems with Appliances:

      ❑ TV

      ❑ Radio/Stereo

      ❑ Computer

      ❑ Clock/Clock Radio

      ❑ Microwave

      ❑ Other: _____

Are there any accounts of paranormal phenomena occuring at occupants' previous residence? If so, explain:

_____

_____

_____

_____

_____

Any history of hoaxing involved with occupant or family member? If yes, explain:

_____

_____

_____

Investigator Impressions of Occupants

(Note: Do not show to occupants.
If they request a copy of the interview, omit this part.)

Overall integrity of occupants. Do the occupants appear sincere in telling their accounts? If no, explain:

_____

_____

_____

_____

_____

Does each recounting of the paranormal events remain consistent? If no, explain:

_____

_____

_____

_____

_____

Do the occupants agree on the events related in the accounts? If no, explain:

_____

_____

_____

_____

_____

Do you believe that any of the occupants would want to perform a hoax for attention in any form? If yes, please explain:

_____

_____

_____

_____

_____

Do you believe that there may be any reason to believe that paranormal accounts may be the result of drug use, psychological conditions, overactive imagination, or dishonesty? If yes, please explain:

_____

_____

_____

_____

_____

Form Three: Research Questions

General Information

Date and Time: _____

Investigator: _____

Location of Haunting: _____

Location of Research Gathered: _____

Location Information

Date Building Constructed: _____

Previous Occupants and Dates of Residence:

_____

_____

_____

Was site build on battlefield or sacred site? If so, explain:

_____

_____

_____

Were there any tragedies or deaths associated with the area? If so, explain:

_____

_____

_____

Has there been any other buildings constructed on the site previous to the current one? If yes, explain:

_____

_____

_____

Any other interesting or anomalous information that may be pertinent to your investigation? If yes, explain:

_____

_____

_____

Form Four: Ghost-Hunter's Checklist

General Information

Date and Time:_____Investigator: _____

Haunting Location: _____

Other Investigators Present: _____

_____

Equipment Checklist

❏ Camera
  ❏ Film, Type:_____
❏ Tape Recorder
  ❏ Audiotape, Type:_____
❏ Batteries
❏ Microwave Radiation Detector

❏ Electromagnetic Detector
❏ Pen/Paper
❏ Thermometer
❏ Compass
❏ Watch/Stopwatch
❏ First Aid Kit

Physical Condition of Location

Rating Key

1	2	3	4	5
Very Much	Somewhat	Average	Not Much	Not at All

1. Does the overall condition of the location appear to be in good repair?

1 2 3 4 5

2. Are there any of the following conditions apparent in the area you are investigating?

Drafty Windows	**1 2 3 4 5**
Creaky/Unstable Floors	**1 2 3 4 5**
Noisy Pipes	**1 2 3 4 5**

Investigator Initial Observation

3. In the area considered haunted by the eyewitnesses, do you notice:

Changes in Temperature	**1 2 3 4 5**
Apparitions	**1 2 3 4 5**
Sensation of Being Watched	**1 2 3 4 5**
Sudden Mood Changes	**1 2 3 4 5**
Discarnate Voices	**1 2 3 4 5**
Electrical Problems	**1 2 3 4 5**
Disappearing Objects	**1 2 3 4 5**
Psychic Impressions	**1 2 3 4 5**

Form Five: Documentation of Paranormal Events

Time: _____ Location: _____ Investigator: _____

Events:

_____

_____

_____

_____

_____

Time: _____ Location: _____ Investigator: _____

Events:

_____

_____

_____

_____

_____

Time: _____ Location: _____ Investigator: _____

Events:

_____

_____

_____

_____

_____

Form Six: Results of Investigation

Time: _____ Location: _____ Investigator: _____

Photographic, recorded, or other evidence? If so, list below:

_____

_____

_____

_____

_____

_____

Any signs found of tampering or dishonesty? (If so, please explain.)

_____

_____

_____

_____

_____

_____

Conclusion of Investigation. Go into as much detail as necessary:

_____

_____

_____

_____

_____

_____

_____

_____

_____

Appendix B
Useful Websites
for Ghost Hunters

Many websites are available on the Internet that provide information for ghost hunters. After carefully examining these sites, I would recommend them as providing information that could be beneficial to your ghost-hunting experiences. These are by far not the only sites that are available on the Internet; new sites dedicated to paranormal studies are being created each day.

There are quite a few benefits for looking for the paranormal in cyberspace. With the Internet, ghost hunters from around the world can converge and discuss their views and beliefs on the paranormal. In addition, ghost hunters can look online for the following purposes.

Compare Accounts

Reports of other paranormal events can be used for case studies to compare to your own ghostly accounts. You can use well-documented accounts as a how-to guide to write your own or to look for similarities in the individual phenomena. Also, in time you will be able to tell the authentic accounts from the fabricated hoaxes. This is a skill that is imperative to have in this line of work.

Spirit Photography

Many websites offer uploaded images of ghosts and spirits from around the world. Quite a few of these are from average people who have unintentionally caught apparitions on their family pictures and a few are taken by paranormal investigators who intentionally have taken these pictures of spirits.

Again, there is one note of caution when you view these photographs. Although many of the pictures may appear to be legitimate, some merely were technical problems with the film or camera (double exposures, moisture on the lens, etc.) or outright hoaxes. It may prove beneficial to periodically look at these pictures to determine if you can distinguish the legitimate from the fake pictures.

Updated Information on Ghosts and Hauntings

Theories on the paranormal are constantly being updated as more information is being uncovered and studied. As we learn more about this phenomenon, more serious research is being conducted and more data is being collected. This in turn allows professionals to offer us accurate theories and hypotheses that may make understanding the nature of ghosts and spirits a bit easier.

Professional Organizations

I would highly recommend joining at least one or two organizations that are offered online. It will increase your integrity and credibility if you belong to a nationally recognized organization. I've found that clients love credentials and memberships; it puts their minds to rest that you belong to a large group of people that are affiliated with a real organization. There are a large number of national paranormal groups online. Careful selection and knowing what you want is very important to find an organization that you can get the most from.

Another way to find additional websites is to simply go to some of the more powerful search engines and type in keywords such as "ghosts," "spirits," "paranormal," etc. Personally, I use search engines such as Metacrawler.com, Dogpile.com, and Lycos.com. However, this is only a matter of personal preference. As always, use what works best for you.

The following is a listing of websites I have personal experience with. Each site has links to many other interesting sites on ghosts and the paranormal.

MAJDA Paranormal Group Website
www.majda.net

This is the official website of one of the most respected and fastest growing paranormal groups in the eastern United States.

Haunted Parkersburg Tours
www.hauntedparkersburg.com

The homepage of Susan Sheppard's wildly popular haunted tour, which has been a success for the last several years.

Moundsville Penitentiary Ghost Hunt
www.wvpentours.com/events.htm

This prison tour offers people the opportunity to periodically explore the halls of the penitentiary looking for paranormal phenomena.

International Ghost Hunters' Society
www.ghostweb.com

The official site of the IGHS offers free membership to anyone interested in the paranormal. It also provides opportunities for classes in ghost hunting, free educational articles on ghost hunting, and many other features. A very good site to learn all about ghost hunting!

Glossary

Apparition: The appearance of a ghost or spirit, usually taking the form of a visual image of a deceased individual in either real life or on film. However, there are apparitions based on each of the five senses. Usually visual, auditory, tactile, or olfactory apparitions appear in conjunction with each other, but occasionally only one of the senses are involved. Very rarely is the sense of taste involved. Examples include:

Visual: The appearance of a person who was commonly associated with the area in life.

Auditory: Sounds of walking, voices, doors, opening, or battle are the most common types of auditory apparitions.

Olfactory: Smells or odors, such as perfume or cigar smoke, commonly associated with the area or an individual or event.

Tactile: Feeling a slight wind in a closed-off room, or a slight tug on a person's clothing with nobody in the immediate vicinity.

Aura: Energy or life force surrounding all living individuals. The color of an aura can determine the mood or physical condition of an individual. Spirits can sometimes use a physical aura for energy, thereby depleting the person whose energy was taken.

Dream Communication: Experience in which the departed individual (spirit) can manifest in the form of a dream in order to communicate with the living. Usually associated with the very recent death of the individual attempting to make contact in order to inform the dreamer of his or her death.

Epicenter: Person or persons that a poltergeist or haunting tends to focus on. Paranormal phenomena usually increases when the epicenter is present.

ESP: Extrasensory perception. Most individuals have this ability, although it can be dormant their entire life. In many cases, a traumatic event may allow a percipient to actually communicate with the spirit of a dead individual.

Ghost: A recording of one or more persons or objects that had either a repetitious routine or a very intense emotional experience. This recording is not sentient, but rather simply something that plays over and over, gradually losing energy over time. This recording can be recharged under certain circumstances, such as the appearance of certain individuals. (See *Epicenter*.)

Ghost Hunter: A person who investigates hauntings to find explanations for possible paranormal phenomena involved. There are two types of ghost hunters. The first kind is the scientific hunter who uses scientific methods and equipment in order to make accurate calculations and observations about a haunting. The second type is the psychic or intuitive ghost hunter, who uses psychic impressions or intuition to learn about a haunted area.

Haunting: Any repeated appearance of phenomena commonly associated with ghosts, spirits, or poltergeists. Usually a combination of cold spots, apparitions, missing objects, and other forms of paranormal activity that tend to be witnessed by more than one person over an extended period of time.

Hoax: A prestaged or preplanned series of events to give the impression that something paranormal has been occurring in any given place. Usually made by people who wish to draw attention to themselves or to debunk or test ghost hunters and parapsychologists.

Manifestation: The tangible signs of a haunting, including tactile, auditory, olfactory, and visual. These can be measured in an investigation and can be used to support the evidence that a place is indeed haunted. (See also *Apparition.*)

Medium: A person who channels a spirit, or through whom a spirit or entity communicates.

Ouija board: A board with letters and numbers on which a planchette (or marker) is placed in order to communicate with the spirits of the dead. Usually used in divination, it can actually be used to summon spirits other than those initially sought after. It is very difficult to rid an area of a spirit that has been conjured through a Ouija board.

Paranormal: Anything out of the normal range of explanation. Term is usually used in conjunction with ghosts, UFOs, and other phenomena that cannot be explained by traditional scientific theories and hypotheses.

Paranormal Group: A group of individuals dedicated to discussing, investigating, or exploring possible explanations to hauntings and other paranormal or supernatural events.

Percipient: An individual involved with or observing a paranormal event.

Poltergeist: German for "noisy ghost." A paranormal manifestation that is generally centered around an individual (usually an adolescent going through puberty) in which objects disappear or are thrown about. The individual the phenomenon is centered around is called the epicenter. There is very little communication between the spirit and the epicenter, and many researchers believe that the cause of the poltergeist is actually latent telekinetic ability rather than an actual spirit.

Possession (of a person by a spirit): The entry of a spirit into the body of a willing or unwilling host, in which the spirit takes control of the individual's motor and cognitive functions.

Psychic Impression: A form of idea or message that a percipient may encounter about an area, a person, or an event. Usually associated with precognition, retrocognition, or psychometry.

Recording: See *Ghost.*

Séance: A meeting of individuals in order to contact the spirit of a deceased loved one or other person (usually consisting of a medium, assistants, loved ones of the departed, or other interested individuals). Many séances were exposed as hoaxes in the late eighteenth and early nineteenth centuries.

Spirit: The actual consciousness or soul of an individual that has passed on and continues to be observed in an area. There are four main reasons that spirits exist: (1) The person does not realize that he or she is dead; (2) there is unfinished business or an unkept promise after death; (3) the spirit is simply saying goodbye to a loved one; and (4) the spirit has returned to offer advice.

Vortex: The center of spiritual energy, where it is focused or concentrated. Usually accompanied by cold spots, electromagnetic disturbances, and increased paranormal activity.

Bibliography

Bodine, Echo. *Relax, It's Only a Ghost.* Boston, Mass.: Element Books, 2000.

Blackman, W. Haden. *The Field Guide to North American Hauntings.* Three Rivers, Calif.: Three Rivers Press, 1998.

Coleman, Christopher K. *Ghosts and Haunts of the Civil War.* Nashville, Tenn.: Rutledge Hill Press, 1999.

Deitz, Dennis. *The Greenbrier Ghost and Other Strange Stories.* Charleston, W. Va.: Quarrier Press, 1990.

Guiley, Rosemary. *The Encyclopedia of Ghosts and Spirits.* New York, N.Y.: Facts on File, 1999.

Hauck, Dennis W. *Haunted Places: The National Directory. A Guidebook to Ghostly Abodes, Sacred Sites, UFO Landings, and Other Supernatural Locations.* New York, N.Y.: Penguin Books, 1996.

Holzer, Hans. *Ghosts, Hauntings, and Possessions: The Best of Hans Holzer, Book I. Vol. 1.* St. Paul, Minn.: Llewellyn Publications, 1990.

————. *Where the Ghosts Are: The Ultimate Guide to Haunted Houses.* New York, N.Y.: Carol Publishing Group, 1995.

Marsden, Simon. *The Haunted Realm: Ghosts, Spirits, and their Uncanny Abodes.* Syracuse, N.Y.: E.P. Dutton, 1987.

Myers, Arthur. *Ghostly American Places.* New York, N.Y.: Random House Value Publishing, 1995.

Mesbitt, Mark V. *Ghosts of Gettysburg: Spirits, Apparitions, and Haunted Places of the Battlefield.* Gettysburg, Pa.: Thomas Publications, 1996.

Ogden, Tom. *The Complete Idiot's Guide to Ghosts and Hauntings.* New York, N.Y.: Macmillian Publishing, 1999.

Robson, Ellen. *Haunted Highway: The Spirits of Route 66.* Phoenix, Ariz.: Golden West Publishers, 1999.

Taylor, Troy. *The Ghost Hunter's Guidebook: The Essential Guide to Investigating Reports of Ghosts and Hauntings.* Alton, Ill.: Taylor Books, 1999.

Wilson, Colin. *Poltergeist: A Study in Destructive Haunting.* St. Paul, Minn.: Llewellyn Publications, 1993.

Index

Grave's End
A True Ghost Story

Elaine Mercado
Foreword by Hans Holzer

When Elaine Mercado and her first husband bought their home in Brooklyn, N.Y., in 1982, they had no idea that they and their two young daughters were embarking on a 13-year nightmare.

Within a few days of moving in, Elaine began to have the sensation of being watched. Soon her oldest daughter Karen felt it too, and they began hearing scratching noises and noticing weird smells. Before long, they were seeing shadowy figures scurry along the baseboards and small balls of light bouncing off the ceilings. In the attic they sometimes saw a very small woman dressed as a bride, and on the stairs they would see a young man. Then the "suffocating dreams" started. Yet her husband refused to sell the house.

This book is the true story of how one family tried to adjust to living in a haunted house. It also tells how, with the help of parapsychologist Dr. Hans Holzer and medium Marisa Anderson, they discovered the identity of the ghosts and were able to assist them to the "light."

0-7387-0003-7, 6 x 9, 192 pp. $12.95

Also available in Spanish
Apariciones
0-7387-0214-5 $12.95

To order by phone call 1-877 NEW WRLD
Prices subject to change without notice

How to Communicate with Spirits

Elizabeth Owens

Spiritualist mediums share their
fascinating experiences with the "other side"

No where else will you find such a wealth of anecdotes from noted professional mediums residing within a Spiritualist community. These real-life psychics shed light on spirit entities, spirit guides, relatives who are in spirit, and communication with all of those on the spirit side of life.

You will explore the different categories of spirit guidance, and you will hear from the mediums themselves about their first contacts with the spirit world, as well as the various phenomena they have encountered.

- Noted mediums residing within a Spiritualist community share their innermost experiences, opinions, and advice regarding spirit communication
- Includes instructions for table tipping, automatic writing, and meditating to make contact with spirits
- For anyone interested in developing and understanding spiritual gifts

1-56718-530-4, 5 3/16 x 8, 240 pp. glossary, bibliog. $9.95

To order by phone call 1-877 NEW WRLD
Prices subject to change without notice

Buckland's Book of Spirit Communications

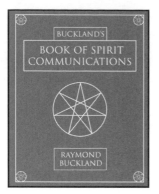

Raymond Buckland

There has been a revival of spiritualism in recent years, with more and more people attempting to communicate with disembodied spirits via talking boards, seances, and other mediums.

Buckland's Book of Spirit Communications is for anyone who wishes to communicate with spirits, as well as for the less adventurous who simply want to satisfy their curiosity about the subject. Explore the nature of the spiritual body and learn how to prepare yourself to become a medium. Experience for yourself the trance state, clairvoyance, psychometry, table tipping, levitation, talking boards, automatic writing, spiritual photography, spiritual healing, distant healing, channeling, and development circles. Also learn how to avoid spiritual fraud.

0-7387-0399-0, 272 , 8 ½ x 11, 272 pp., illus.   **$12.95**

Spirit of Love
A Medium's Message of Life Beyond Death

Jenny Crawford

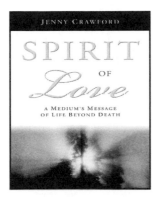

A spiritual medium shares compelling case studies of the world that awaits us after death, of soul rescue work, of the spirit world orchestrating meetings with departed loved ones, and how we can all be conduits of spirit.

A question and answer chapter covers everything from what it means to be clairvoyant, to the role of free will, to the various levels of the spirit world. Includes an account of the late singer Karen Carpenter.

0-7387-0273-0, 5 3/16 x 8, 240 pp.   **$12.95**

Also available in Spanish
Contacto espiritual
0-7387-0289-7   **$14.95**

To order by phone call 1-877 NEW WRLD
Prices subject to change without notice

True Hauntings
Spirits with a Purpose

Hazel M. Denning, Ph.D.

Do spirits feel and think? Does death automatically promote them to a paradise—or as some believe, a hell? Real-life ghostbuster Dr. Hazel M. Denning reveals the answers through case histories of the friendly and hostile earthbound spirits she has encountered. Learn the reasons spirits remain entrapped in the vibrational force field of the earth: fear of going to the other side, desire to protect surviving loved ones, and revenge. Dr. Denning also shares fascinating case histories involving spirit possession, psychic attack, mediumship, and spirit guides. Find out why spirits haunt us in *True Hauntings,* the only book of its kind written from the perspective of the spirits themselves.

1-56718-218-6, 6 x 9,240 pp. $12.95

What Happens After Death
Scientific & Personal Evidence for Survival

Migene González-Wippler

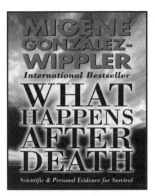

What does science tell us about life after death? How do the different religions explain the mystery? What is the answer given by the strange mystical science known as Spiritism? These and other questions about the life beyond are explored in *What Happens After Death.*

The first part of the book is an objective study of the research about life after death. The second part is a personal narrative by a spirit guide named Kirkudian about his various incarnations. While the two sections could be considered two separate books, they simply express the same concepts in uniquely different ways.

Experience for yourself one soul's journey through the afterlife, and discover the ultimate truth: that every soul is created in union with all other souls, and that we are all manifestations of one purpose.

1-56718-327-1, 5 ³⁄₁₆ x 8, 256 pp. $7.95

Also available in Spanish
Peregrinaje
1-56718-330-1 $9.95

To order by phone call 1-877 NEW WRLD
Prices subject to change without notice

Death:
Beginning or End?
Methods for Immortality

Dr. Jonn Mumford

This book is an exhilarating celebration of life—and death. It is a thought-provoking and interactive tool that will alter your perceptions about death and prepare you for reincarnation. Explore the history of death rituals and attitudes from other ages and cultures. Uncover surprising facts about this inevitable life event. Moreover, discover the ultimate truth about death, knowledge that is guaranteed to have a profound impact on how you live the rest of your life!

Learn how your experience of life after birth will impact your experience of life after death. Personally engage in five "alchemical laboratories"—five of the most crucial "stocktaking" exercises you will ever do. Learn a traditional Hindu meditation that will provide a psychic and mental refuge as well as deep physical relaxation. Practice a mantra that can liberate you from the endless wheel of blind incarnation. Use the tools provided in the book and avoid the death's biggest tragedy: to not ever discover who you are in life.

1-56718-476-6, 5 ³⁄₁₆ x 6, 224 pp. $9.95

Journey of Souls
Case Studies of Life Between Lives

Michael Newton, Ph.D.

This remarkable book uncovers—for the first time—the mystery of life in the spirit world after death on earth. Dr. Michael Newton, a hypnotherapist in private practice, has developed his own hypnosis technique to reach his subjects' hidden memories of the hereafter. The narrative is woven as a progressive travel log around the accounts of twenty-nine people who were placed in a state of superconsciousness. While in deep hypnosis, these subjects describe what has happened to them between their former reincarnations on earth. They reveal graphic details about how it feels to die, who meets us right after death, what the spirit world is really like, where we go and what we do as souls, and why we choose to come back in certain bodies.

After reading *Journey of Souls,* you will acquire a better understanding of the immortality of the human soul. Plus, you will meet day-to-day personal challenges with a greater sense of purpose as you begin to understand the reasons behind events in your own life.

1-56718-485-5, 6 x 9, 288 pp. $14.95

Destiny of Souls
New Case Studies of
Life Between Lives

Michael Newton, Ph.D.

A pioneer in uncovering the secrets of life, internationally recognized spiritual hypnotherapist Dr. Michael Newton takes you once again into the heart of the spirit world. His groundbreaking research was first published in the best-selling *Journey of Souls*, the definitive study on the afterlife. Now, in *Destiny of Souls*, the saga continues with seventy case histories of real people who were regressed into their lives between lives. Dr. Newton answers the requests of the thousands of readers of the first book who wanted more details about various aspects of life on the other side. *Destiny of Souls* is also designed for the enjoyment of first-time readers who haven't read *Journey of Souls*. Hear the stories of people in deep hypnosis as they tell about:

- Ways spirits connect with and comfort the living
- Spirit guides and the council of wise beings who interview us after each life
- Who is a soulmate and linkages between soul groups and human families
- The soul-brain connection and why we choose certain bodies

1-56718-499-5, 6 x 9, 384 pp., illus. $14.95